DATE DUE	
DEC 14 1970	
AUG 1 1973	
APR 22 '81	
8/24/81	
5/8r	

GAYLORD M-2   PRINTED IN U.S.A.

The Journalistic Interview

The
JOURNALISTIC
INTERVIEW

by Hugh C. Sherwood

HARPER & ROW, PUBLISHERS
New York, Evanston, and London

FIRST EDITION

LIBRARY OF CONGRESS CATALOG CARD NUMBER: 75-81882

To Carli

Contents

Preface

When I graduated from the Columbia University School of Journalism two decades ago I was, I hope, a reasonably good writer. I think I also had some sense of what was news and what wasn't.

As I look back on it now, however, I was not a good interviewer. To some extent I realized this even then. Lack of experience and practice were, I suppose, the chief reasons.

Three of the next four years I spent in military service. Fortunately, my assignments were such that I was able to put much of what I had learned at Columbia to worthwhile use. I was even able to do some interviewing.

In any case, not too many months after my service had ended I had cocktails with a newfound friend—an older woman who had had experience in several facets of journalism. Among other things, she had written some cookbooks. And during a lull in the conversation I asked her how one went about writing a cookbook. One question led to another and, about ten minutes later, she quietly told me I was an excellent interviewer.

I suppose there are a few times in every man's life when

someone says just the right thing to him at just the right time. For me, that was one of those times.

This is not to say that I have not learned much about interviewing in subsequent years. I have learned a great deal. In fact, most of the precepts and some of the anecdotes in this book are based on this subsequent experience. To a lesser degree, I have drawn on casual professional conversations with fellow journalists and on occasional readings of what others have had to say about the art of interviewing, although, surprisingly, less has been written about it than you might think.

Nonetheless, I would be remiss if I did not give special thanks where special thanks is due. One must go to Richard E. Mooney, a long-time friend, for giving me the benefit of his thinking about off-the-record interviews, to supplement my own. These are discussed in Chapter 7. Dick once served in New York City and Washington, D.C., with United Press (now United Press International) and later in the Washington and Paris Bureaus of the *New York Times*. Presently he is special assistant to James Reston, the *Times* executive editor. I also wish to thank Wallace D. Huskonen, technical editor of *Foundry* magazine, for allowing me to draw on his up-to-the-minute knowledge of the present state of development of the tape recorder, which is discussed in Chapter 5. Finally, I wish to thank Mrs. Sandra Covello for typing the manuscript for this book and, more important, for telling me that it was interesting. I hope you find it so too.

Pleasantville, N.Y.   HUGH C. SHERWOOD

1. Who Are You Anyway?

Someday, for the fun of it, stop a United States Marine on the street and ask him what his job is. Chances are seven out of ten that he will answer "Rifleman."

It won't matter whether he commands a company, a platoon, or only himself. It won't matter that he may actually be a photographer, a cartographer, or a staff aide to the Commandant of the Marine Corps. Nor will it matter that a rifleman has the lowest, grubbiest, most dangerous job in the Marine Corps. The chances are still good that—be he corporal, captain, or colonel—the Marine will tell you that he's a rifleman.

The reason is simple. The Marines are trained to believe that their first, last, and most important job is to fight. They do most of their fighting on the ground. And on the ground the rifle is still this country's basic weapon.

The world of journalism is very wide. It includes newspapers, magazines, radio, television, public opinion polling, public relations, and many subdivisions of all these functions.

Like the Marine Corps, it has its colonels, captains and corporals. They merely bear such titles as editor or associate editor or columnist or director of public relations.

1

Whatever tasks these men actually perform, however, the best of them have never forgotten that their basic job is still the lowest—and the most important—in the field of journalism. They realize that that job is reporting. They know that, whatever their present tasks, they may be asked at any time to interview people, pore through records, and come up with a report that disseminates information that will be considered interesting, important, or useful—and, hopefully, all three.

Facts, information, knowledge reach these men, these reporters, in many ways. It may come through the pages of a competing publication. It may come through an annual report to a company's stockholders. It may come through encyclopedias or reference books. It may come through tips from friends or acquaintances. It may come through telephone calls. It may come through personal observation. It may come through press releases.

Yet the most important information they receive comes directly from other people. It comes through interviewing these people, face to face, for a few minutes or a few hours or even a few days.

Interviewing is no easy job. At its best it requires that the reporter make a careful choice of the person or persons he interviews so that he may obtain the most authoritative opinion possible on the subject at hand. In many cases it also requires that the reporter do careful advance reading on the subject he wants to talk about so that he will waste neither his own time nor that of the person he is interviewing, and so that he may go beyond basic, obvious questions and investigate the subject in depth. Obviously, it also requires a careful choice of questions, a careful listening to answers, a careful taking of notes, and a careful, objective report on what has been said and seen.

The best interviews usually take place in the office or the home of the man who is interviewed. Hopefully, that man has had several days' advance notice that he will be interviewed and some notion of what the reporter who will interview him wants to know. Hopefully, too, both the reporter and the man he interviews will have some time at their disposal—at least an hour, preferably two or three, possibly many more.

Not all interviews take place under such ideal conditions. Sometimes they must be conducted over lunch tables or in taxicabs or on street corners. Sometimes neither the reporter nor the person who is being interviewed has much, if any, advance word that the interview will take place. Sometimes the interview must be conducted in the space of a few minutes rather than in the space of a few hours.

Nonetheless, contrary to what you may think, the best reporter is not necessarily the man who can ask six or seven rapid-fire questions on the steps of a state capitol building or in the hallways of a court of justice, then run for the nearest telephone. Rather, it is the other way around.

The best reporter is usually the man who can ask 160 or 170 questions over the space of a few hours, then write a coherent, organized, interesting report on what he has learned. Hopefully, he will have several hours or days to do the job. But if not, he will be able to turn out his story on short notice.

Until he died a few years ago, the *New York Times* boasted one of this country's all-time great reporters. His name was Meyer Berger and, at one time or another, he covered almost every kind of story you could think of. In fact, the *Times* thought so highly of him that it assigned him to write its 100-year history, *The Story of The New York Times: 1851–1951*.

Berger hated the job. Although he did it brilliantly, he did it reluctantly. He longed to be back on the street, gathering stories for the daily newspaper.

Happily, one September day he was given a brief respite from his historical labors. A man named Howard Unruh had run amok in Camden, New Jersey, killing twelve people in only twenty minutes' time. Since most of its other ablest reporters were already out on assignment, the *Times* sent Berger.

I heard him tell once, in his diffident, almost halting way, how he had done the job. He had gone to Camden and interviewed almost everybody he could—police, people who had observed some of the killings, friends and relatives of the victims. He had even retraced the actual path the killer had taken and studied his war-souvenir-littered bedroom.

It took Berger many hours to gather the information he needed and, when he got back to the *Times* offices on New York's West 43rd Street, he had only ninety minutes to write his story. What he wrote took up all of one column on the *Times* front page and several more columns on an inside page—a total of several thousand words. It won him a Pulitzer Prize.

To gather his material Berger had to conduct many off-the-cuff interviews. But the man who would master the art of conducting this kind of interview will first master the art of conducting the long, involved, detailed interview. He will learn to ask many questions—both those that he has come prepared to ask and those that naturally occur to him during the course of the. interview. He will learn to weed out the useful and important answers from the trivial and the irrelevant. He will learn to write a story that leaves no important questions unanswered in either his own or his readers' minds.

If he will learn to do these things and learn to do them well, then it will become second nature to him to conduct the quick, unexpected interview. By instinct he will know the ten or twelve key questions he must ask. By instinct he will know whether he has enough interesting information for an article or not.

Whatever title you hold, whatever title you hope to hold in the world of journalism, you are then, first of all, a reporter. And to be a good reporter you must first of all be a good interviewer. Just how, you may wonder, can you become one?

Like men in every other profession, journalists have learned some techniques for making the most of an interview. Although these techniques are often simple, they are also effective.

For example, if a person fails to answer a question, it is often enough to ask him the question again. Or if he wants to answer a question off the record, it is sometimes enough to stop him in mid-sentence and tell him that you can get an on-the-record answer from another source.

I'll have more to say about techniques like these later on. What must be emphasized here is that no techniques, no tricks, no ploys will substitute for the impression you make as a person. Despite the thrill that some people feel at the prospect of being interviewed by a journalist, despite the suspicion, even hostility, that others exhibit, they will ultimately respond to you not as a journalist but as another human being. Make a good impression and, if the person whom you are interviewing is intelligent and informed about the subject at hand, you should get a good interview. Make a poor impression and you will fail—or at least come away with less than you might have.

How can you make a good impression? It's not very

different from making a good impression in any other undertaking.

For one thing, you can be friendly. It's not necessary—it's usually not even wise—to meet the person you are going to interview with a beaming smile and a pumping handshake. Such exaggerated glad-handing may get you nowhere.

But a simple smile, a quick, firm handshake, and a direct gaze are called for. If I seem to mention the obvious, I do so with a purpose. Many people are just a little apprehensive at a first or even a second interview with a journalist and, therefore, just a little guarded. I have known this to be true even of people who have been highly successful and well known in their professions.

One reason isn't hard to guess at. Being interviewed is new to them. They want to make a good impression. And yet they're going up against something unknown to them—you and, more particularly, the questions you'll ask of them.

Then, too, journalism has had in its ranks people who have given it, if not a bad name, then a poorer one than it should have. Most people have read about, heard about, or actually seen a hard-driving reporter who has virtually backed some poor individual against a wall and subjected him to a veritable third degree before letting him go.

In short, anything you can do to indicate to the person you are about to interview that you are friendly and well disposed will help you. If nothing else, it will put him at his ease. And that is the very first step to a successful interview.

For another thing, you can be intelligent. Unfortunately, but perhaps unavoidably, the person whom you interview may judge your intelligence in terms of your knowledge of his own trade or profession. If you know—or seem to know—something about it, he will be more apt to let down his guard and tell you things he might otherwise withhold.

Of course, being well informed about the profession of the person you are interviewing may not always be possible. You may be assigned to interview someone on a subject you know next to nothing about. Even so, you may be able to read up on the subject before the interview and familiarize yourself with it in a general way. You can at least remember the basic questions that must be asked in almost every interview. I refer, of course, to Kipling's famous lines: "I keep six honest serving men/ (They taught me all I knew);/ Their names are What and Why and When/ And How and Where and Who." I refer, too, to such questions as: What are the benefits of this development (event, decision)? What are the drawbacks? What are the likely results?

Finally, you can avoid questions that deal merely with the trivial or the irrelevant. Show by your initial statement of purpose and your subsequent line of questioning that you are aiming at an intelligent goal, and you will inevitably draw the person you are interviewing along with you.

If it's important that you be friendly and intelligent when you interview, it's also important that you avoid being a pushover for vague generalizations, evasions, and statements that are merely self-serving. There are, to be sure, times when it is wise to overlook a man's evasion or the self-serving nature of the information he gives you. This is certainly likely to be the case if he is, in general, providing excellent answers to your questions and if, furthermore, you have reason to believe that any attempt to bring him up short would end the interview or result in poorer answers to your further questions.

But cases like these are the exception rather than the

rule. In general people are not impressed with journalists who seem callow, inexperienced, uninformed, easily put off—or too easily answered. Never let yourself appear in such a light.

Not long ago I had occasion to interview a man about profit sharing and other ways of providing people with compensation over and above their ordinary salaries. He was an intelligent man, well spoken, an expert in his field. But he was also an exponent of profit sharing, and I was not there to learn about the merits of profit sharing but to gain some basic factual information about it and to obtain an objective appraisal of it in relation to other methods of so-called incentive compensation. Before ten or twelve minutes had passed, however, it became apparent that he was slanting his answers ever so slightly in favor of profit sharing.

I waited for his answers to another question or two, then asked him about a certain company that had suffered a strike as a direct result of its profit-sharing plan. Obviously, my question implied that profit sharing had drawbacks as well as advantages.

His face suddenly froze. He spread his hands palms down on the desk. And then, in an instant, he relaxed. His whole attitude changed. He began answering questions about profit sharing much more honestly and frankly than before, and he continued to do so throughout the interview.

I did not know as much about profit sharing as he did. I still do not. But I had let him know, by a single question, that I knew more about it than he thought I did. As a result, a whole interview was changed.

Finally, if you are to be a successful interviewer, you must impress the people you interview as a decent human being as well as a good journalist. I know of no way you can accomplish this unless you treat them as human beings.

One way to do this is to treat them with reasonable courtesy. In our informal country, in an increasingly informal age, people very quickly get on a first-name basis. This, of course, has great advantages. But in many interviews it can be fatal to assume that you may address a man or a woman by his or her first name the very first moment you meet. In short, although it's wise to be relaxed and friendly, you will usually do well to let the person you are interviewing take the lead in putting your relationship on an informal basis. In the long run, I think, you will find that this approach will pay.

Another thing you can do is to show reasonable respect to the person you are interviewing. This does not mean that you should be deferential. In fact, if you are deferential, you will only put yourself at a disadvantage. The person you interview will assume that you think he is doing you a great favor in letting you interview him. He may even assume an attitude of noblesse oblige. The frankness and openness you had hoped for will disappear.

There are times in interviewing when it is necessary to be argumentative. There are even occasions when it is necessary to be rude. But these occasions are rare. If you will show reasonable respect to the person you interview, you will, in most cases, not be argumentative nor rude, no matter how wild his person, his attitudes, or his opinions may seem to you. Rather, you will take down his remarks as faithfully as you can. And if you would impress him with your sense of responsibility, you may occasionally ask him to repeat a fact or a remark so that you can be sure you have taken it down correctly.

If you are a reporter, you must be an interviewer. And if

you are to be a good interviewer, you must impress most of
the people you interview as friendly, intelligent, not easily
maneuvered—and, above all, as a human being who can be
talked with as another human being and not just as a journalist.

The impressions you give cannot be faked. They must be
part of you. For the very circumstances of your work will
reveal many, many times whether they are part of you or
not.

A few years ago I got to know a charming young man
who had drifted out of law school and into journalism.
After a few years of varied work, he had joined the staff of
a magazine whose name is a household word in most American homes. He had not joined as a writer, but as a researcher whose reports would be used by other journalists
as a basis for finished articles. He seemed to have a knack
for gathering facts and, because of his relaxed, merry way,
an even greater knack for establishing easy rapport with
other people. In fact, he got them to tell him things that
they did not seem to tell other journalists.

One day he was assigned to interview a nationally known
woman singer and entertainer. The interview went swim-
mingly. In fact, after two or three hours of steady conversation she went so far as to confess to the young man that she
was sexually frigid.

He asked a question or two, then went onto other matters. Not long afterwards he ended the interview.

At three o'clock the following morning, he received a
desperate telephone call from the woman. He would not,
she asked, mention that she was sexually frigid, would
he?

The young man said he would. The woman entertainer
begged him not to and, when he balked, she pleaded—and

even wept. But the young researcher was firm. She had given him the information. And he would report it.

The young man may well have been in the wrong. At least his editors seemed to think so. They had her confession on tape and could probably easily have withstood a libel suit. Nonetheless, they chose never to report her confession.

The point is not that the young man was wrong—or right. The point is that, if you ever interview any great number of people, you, too, will be tested as a human being. You will have the power to report—or not to report —their actions, their hopes, their fears, their frustrations, and their shames.

Sometimes you will be faced with requests to delete or change statements they have made to you. Sometimes you will be faced with requests to add to what they have said. Sometimes the requests will be trivial, irrelevant, or ego-tistical. Sometimes they will be weighty, pertinent, and modest. Sometimes they will be made matter-of-factly, sometimes plaintively, sometimes threateningly.

Sometimes it will not be an editor who will have the final say as to whether the request is honored. Because of lack of time, force of circumstance, or greater over-all knowledge of the situation you are writing about, the decision will lie with you.

And when it does, you will feel some of the power of the press and sense that you hold part of that power. You will know that, to one person or to several persons or to a whole organization or even to a whole government, you are, for that moment in time, a very important man. Just how im-portant? That is a subject worth looking at more closely.

2. How Important Are You?

In England newspaper reporting is not a glamorous profession. The reporter is not looked up to, and he is often looked down on.

England, of course, is still class conscious, and the newspaper reporter does not usually wear an old school tie. Then, too, the English revere personal privacy to an extent that Americans do not, and the reporter is an actual or potential invader of that privacy.

Although much may be said against the status of the journalist in America, he is not looked down upon. And the bigger and better known the communications medium he represents—newspaper, magazine, or whatever—the more likely it is that he will be looked up to.

When all this began it is hard to say, but it may have been with the coming to power of the administration of Franklin D. Roosevelt. Important, different, and exciting things began happening in Washington in those days, and the Roosevelt Administration was freer than its predecessors had been in telling the press what it was doing. Roosevelt was a master of the communications media, and he knew he needed the press to tell the American people where he wanted the country to go.

Furthermore, there arose in those days the great columnists—the semiomniscient commentators on affairs great and small, who seemed to look on political events and administrations from a long way off and view them by the standards of the gods. Hard on their heels came some of the great World War II correspondents and then the television newscasters. The result is that, if you will ask today's American what he thinks of when he thinks of a journalist, he may be as apt to answer Eric Sevareid or David Brinkley or James Reston as he is the hard-bitten, hard-driving, hard-drinking newspaperman once made famous by Hollywood.

Journalism may not stand so great in the eyes of Americans as the law, medicine, or certain other callings, but it stands great enough. It is a glamorous profession, and it is likely to remain so for a long time to come. This glamour rubs off, to at least some degree, on all who practice it, and the closer one gets to New York City the more the glamour gleams.

Moving in this world of headlines and deadlines, of cables and microphones, it is easy enough to lose perspective. It is easy to become cynical. It is even easier to become self-important. It is easiest of all to forget that, no matter how well you speak or write, you are still only a conveyer of information, a catalyst, a middleman between sources of information and the vast reading or viewing public.

Yet this must not be forgotten. If it is, any one of several possible serious errors may result.

For one thing, the interviewer may forget one of the rarely voiced but cardinal rules of modern journalism. That is simply this: Almost all articles that appear in newspapers or magazines, and all reports that are purveyed over radio and television, are based on some authority. The authority may be a President of the United States or the head of some foreign land. He may be a medical specialist, a nuclear physicist, or a Broadway star. It does not matter who he is. What does matter is that his comments are, almost by definition, more important than how the interviewer reports those comments.

This is not to say that an interviewer should not strive to make his article or his story as interesting as he possibly can. It is to say that, regardless of how well written or spoken the article or story may be, there would have been no article or story if the person who was interviewed were not important, were not an authority in his field.

The interviewer who forgets this is liable to place himself first, his story second, and the person whom he interviews third. Such a subtle shift in attitude cannot help but be felt by the person being interviewed. And the interviewer who holds this attitude over a long period of time is bound to wind up with interviews that are considerably less successful than they might have been.

Yet this attitude abounds more than is commonly recognized. During the 1960 presidential campaign in particular —but both earlier and later as well—Richard M. Nixon was the victim of just such an attitude on the part of some of the American press. He was frequently subjected to overtly hostile questioning by various reporters who covered his campaigns.

I do not wish to undermine what I am saying by giving the impression that I was a supporter of Nixon in 1960. In fact, I was not. Nor do I wish to leave the impression that Nixon was blameless. He may well not have been.

Nonetheless, newspapers and magazines themselves reported that Nixon was the subject of plainly unfriendly questioning—and of unfriendly stories. Some reporters had put themselves—that is, their own feelings toward Nixon and their own opinions of his political views—first, their stories second, Nixon third, and the American public last. Almost assuredly both the reporters and the public were losers.

It is plain, then, that failure to remember that the person being interviewed is usually the most important aspect of a story is frequently compounded by another error: lack of objectivity. And this error can work both ways. Just as an interviewer can be subtly or overtly hostile to the source of his story, so can he be subtly or overtly too sympathetic or too enthusiastic. The results can be disastrous for responsible journalism.

Several years before he wrote *The Death of a President,* the contents of which the Kennedy family tried so hard to amend, William Manchester wrote another book about John F. Kennedy. It was called *Portrait of a President,* and it was extremely well written. But it was so blatantly laudatory and uncritical of Kennedy that it was sarcastically dismissed by more than one reviewer. It was plain that it would never hold a favored place in the annals of journalism, biography, or history.

Lack of objectivity can sometimes be an even more insidious danger if the interviewer talks with someone he does not know and about whom he has no preconceived opinions. The danger may be greatest with someone who is tremendously enthusiastic about his work. This kind of person usually makes the very best kind of person to interview. His eyes light up. The words roll off his tongue as he tells of his work with the gusto that only the truly dedicated professional can bring. Before the interviewer knows it, he may assess the man's work as much more important than it actually is.

What I am saying, then, is that, no matter how casual and friendly the interviewer may be, he must maintain a certain objectivity, a certain inner detachment, about the person and subject he is writing about. Yet this is easier said than done.

We are all people before we are journalists or polltakers or public relations men. And we carry our prejudices with us. Some of them are part of the very warp and woof of our own profession.

Take the simple matter of the colorful statement. By instinct every journalist likes to interview the man who speaks vividly and memorably—who is, as the saying goes, eminently quotable. In fact, it is easy enough to assume that the man who does not speak in this manner is somehow less interesting and less important than the man who does.

Yet most journalists have found by practical experience that this is almost never so. The ability to phrase things felicitously or colorfully is a wonderful gift. But it should not be assumed that the man who has this gift necessarily has a wealth of information at his disposal or a wealth of sound ideas either. Nor should it be assumed that the man who phrases matters in an ordinary way does not have a great deal of importance to say.

As an interviewer you will inevitably be tempted to judge people inwardly in other ways, too. They may seem too aristocratic and formal or too casual and easygoing. They may seem of great importance or of little importance in the hierarchies of life. They may seem too this or too that.

What's more, the whole problem will be compounded by the fact that you will, by the very nature of your assignments, be compelled to judge the people you interview—at least in certain ways. Do they seem truthful? Objective? Knowledgeable? You will inevitably be making inward assessments on these and related matters during the course of your interviews—and afterwards.

But resist the temptation to judge your interviewees as

people, unless it is part of your assignment to judge them. For your attitude will inevitably creep into your interviewing and into the story you write—usually to both your detriment and that of your readers. Such subjective slanting can throw a whole article out of balance. And a sense of balance, a sense of proportion, in reporting on the affairs of the world is, in a sense, what journalism is all about—and what it needs a great deal more of.

What I have been saying is that you must place yourself —your ego, your opinions, your feelings—last in an interview. You must place the person you are interviewing and the subject you are interviewing him about first.

If you do not believe that this is the wise course—or if you find it difficult to maintain an inward objectivity—give yourself a little test from time to time. Take some subject you know nothing about. Don't take nuclear physics or some subject most other people don't know much about either. Take a subject that many other people know a great deal about, but about which you know next to nothing.

Take cars. A great many American men know a great deal about cars. Some of them could even do a fair job of taking a car apart and putting it together again. Yet you might be at a total loss if you had to distinguish between a piston and a gasket.

Or take football. Most American men know a lot about the game. They know its lingo—safety blitzes, red-dogging, square-outs, and so forth—as well as they know the backs of their own hands. Again, you may know little.

But just suppose that you had to interview a topflight mechanic on the chief differences between the cars of five years ago and those of today. Or suppose you had to interview a topflight football coach on the differences in the way football is played today from the way it was played a decade ago. Who would be more important—you and your opinions of the man you interview or the man and his opinions about the subject at hand?

Perhaps you think I am pointing to a nonexistent danger. The fact is, it is a fundamental danger. It is part of the fact that you and I are human beings. Take this example: A few years ago a friend of mine was employed by a consulting firm. While he was away on a trip the firm decided that all its employees should be given psychological tests. When my friend returned to his offices, another executive took him to lunch, presented him with a list of five companies that gave psychological tests, and told him to choose one—any one—and then arrange to take its test.

My friend chose three. "No, you don't understand," said the other executive. "You're supposed to choose only one."

"I will take three tests or none," my friend replied. "Here is what I am going to do. To the first psychological test I am going to wear a black suit, a black tie, and a black homburg. I am going to carry a black attaché case, and I am going to be smoking a black pipe. To the second psychological test I am going to wear a blue blazer, gray flannels, an ascot, and a sporty pocket handkerchief. And I am going to carry a cane. To the third interview I am going to wear corduroy trousers, a turtleneck sweater with egg spattered on the front of it, and a beat-up sport coat with elbow patches. I will obviously be in need of a haircut."

"But why?" the other executive asked: "I don't get it."

"It's quite simple," my friend replied. "The tests are obviously very similar, or you wouldn't have given me a choice of five tests. So the only thing that can differ is the psychologist who interprets those tests and his impression of me."

The upshot of the story was simple. The plan was reported to the highest level of the company, and a few days later my friend received a call from the president. The president quietly said that psychological testing had been canceled throughout the firm.

By now you may be thinking that you, the interviewer, are not at all important to the success of your interviews. Nothing could be further from the truth.

In fact, I think it is safe to say that, if an interview fails, the fault will be yours in 95 cases out of 100. There are instances, to be sure, in which people are by nature overly taciturn, in which they have not allotted enough time to be interviewed, or when for some other reason the interview fails through no fault of yours.

But these cases should be the exception rather than the rule. Provided you have chosen the person you are to interview with some care, provided you have familiarized yourself with the subject you are to talk about to at least a reasonable degree, and provided you have prepared your questions with precision, you should normally get a good interview, no matter whom you talk to. By good, I don't necessarily mean that a single interview will be sufficient for an article, although that may often be the case. I do mean that the interview will make a reasonabie contribution to the total article or report you have to make.

How important are you? You are very important. Without you, there would be no interview at all. Without thought and preparation on your part, there would very likely not be a good interview. But you must view your role in perspective. You are basically conveying interesting information, important information, or both to an audience of readers or viewers. You are a catalyst, a man who draws out the opinions, the views of another man or woman. The sooner your realization of this fact becomes an instinctive part of your approach the more successful your interviews will be.

3. *How to Get an Interview*

How do you get an interview? The answer to this question would seem simple enough. You ask personally, write to or telephone the person whom you want to interview. You tell him who you are, what you want, and why you want it.

Often enough this simple answer is the correct one. And often enough it isn't. Sometimes, in fact, you'll be wise to approach the person you want to interview through a third party.

This is especially likely to be the case if you want to interview a businessman. In fact, you may take it as a rule of thumb that, if a company is big enough to have a public relations department, you'll probably be wise to work through it rather than approach the executive you want to interview directly.

It's part of a public relations executive's job to facilitate contact with the press. What's more, he's much more apt to perceive the value of publicity for his company than most other executives are.

For proof, some years ago I was assigned to write a story on how companies went about picking new presidents when they chose them from within their own ranks. It seemed

20

logical to assume—and the assumption proved correct—that the men who had just served as presidents and who were now becoming chairmen of their boards had played a major role in selecting their successors.

I decided to interview six presidents-turned-chairmen. But to get six interviews I had to approach 21 companies. What was wrong with the 15 companies that turned me down? In 13 instances the public relations director tentatively agreed to an interview, then was vetoed by his new chairman. Usually it was because the chairman was wary of offending men who had been passed over for the presidency.

The point isn't that many chairmen refused to be interviewed on this subject. The point is that many of their public relations directors thought they should be. The chairmen were wary of publicity. The public relations men weren't.

Naturally this isn't always the case. Much depends on the subject on which you want to hold an interview. Much depends on a particular company's policies and on its fortunes at a particular point in time. Much depends, too, on the kind of executive you want to talk with. Sales executives, for instance, are generally much more willing to be interviewed than treasurers and controllers. By nature and function the former are gregarious and outgoing. The latter are cautious and secretive.

In other words, you can sometimes obtain an interview with no trouble at all by approaching an executive directly. But, generally speaking, you'll do well to approach the men who are charged with obtaining publicity and goodwill for their firms—the public relations people. This rule holds particularly true when you want to talk with someone at a high level in a big firm. At a lower level in a smaller firm—even one with a public relations department—it's often a toss-up as to how best to proceed.

If going through established channels is often wise in business, it's even wiser in politics. During World War II the British Prime Minister, Winston Churchill, made frequent trips to Washington, D.C., to confer with President Franklin D. Roosevelt. Twice while Churchill was in Washington an editor I know was able to interview him on an exclusive basis. One of the interviews resulted in a story that produced headlines all over the world.

Did the editor approach Churchill directly? Obviously, it would have been extremely difficult to get at a man of his stature at any time. In wartime it would have been virtually impossible. Fortunately, the editor knew the British Ambassador to the United States, and the latter arranged the interviews with ease.

At lower political levels, too, the indirect approach is usually best. Senators and congressmen are busy men. If they aren't on the floor of Congress—and they often aren't—they may be out on the hustings making a speech or off in some foreign land conducting an investigation. Unless you're a Washington correspondent who is well known to them, you'll usually do best to approach their administrative assistants. This assumes that you want to talk with a senator or congressman at some length and not just ask him a few questions as he leaves the floor of Congress.

What's true in big business and in politics is even more true in the military. It's virtually impossible to get to see a high-ranking general or admiral at the Pentagon without going through a public information officer. And if you interview an officer of lower rank, what he tells you may have to be cleared through the public information office before it can be published. In general, the armed forces are stricter than most business firms have ever thought of being about who speaks to whom—and about what.

Out in the field, at the military posts around the country,

things are a little less strict, but not much. Captains and colonels may sometimes be willing and able to talk about their posts' athletic teams or the morale of their men or the nature of the training these men are getting, without checking with higher authority. But they are unlikely to talk about anything meaty without making sure you have obtained clearance.

In combat zones resourceful reporters have sometimes been able to take officers or enlisted men aside and obtain a truer picture of the progress of a particular battle or the number of dead and wounded than any public information officer has been willing to give them. But these reporters have had to work with discretion, both for the sake of the men they interview and for their own. The military has ways of retaliating against reporters who go outside official channels, then print something it doesn't like.

Thus, in 1968, during the Vietnam War, a correspondent for the Baltimore *Sun* went to the battle area around Khesanh, which only a few months previously American troops had fought hard and successfully to hold. He saw that the Americans were abandoning the post and, believing that the enemy could see what was happening, he reported the abandonment in his newspaper.

In so doing he violated a ground rule for press coverage of the war. This rule stipulated that the press could not report movement of American troops without clearance from the military. This and some fifteen other ground rules had been established by the armed forces in lieu of outright censorship.

As a result of his report, the correspondent lost his military accreditation card for two months and was put on probation for another four. This effectively prevented him from talking with either military or diplomatic officials, and it also barred him from using military transportation.

Actors and actresses are more nonconformist than many other people. Besides, they are often located far from the organizations with which they are officially connected. Thus they may be appearing in plays on Broadway rather than working on a movie lot in Hollywood. For these two reasons they can sometimes be approached directly. Even so, they often have ties with studios or are represented by press agents. These organizations and people have a vested interest in getting their stars publicity. So here, too, it is often wise to work through established channels.

What about the millions of people who have no public relations executives, no administrative assistants, no public information officers, and no press agents? How do you get interviews with them? By approaching them directly.

It's getting easier to do, and it should get easier yet. The main reason is the rise of the on-the-spot television reporter. In recent years millions have watched these reporters roam among crowds after racial or other kinds of riots and ask questions of people sometimes picked at random. This kind of reporting has accustomed the TV viewers to seeing people just like themselves talk freely and naturally with reporters. As a result, I think, the future will find people less reluctant to become involved with the press.

This will not be true in all cases, of course. People who are in trouble—or who have friends and relatives in trouble —can often be as closed-mouthed as a Vermont farmer. For example, in 1968, shortly after it was announced that James Earl Ray was wanted for the assassination of Dr. Martin Luther King, the Negro civil rights leader, reporters from *Life* fanned out through the Midwest in an effort to talk with anyone who had ever known Ray.

The chief of *Life*'s Chicago Bureau later reported: "The competition was terrific. We were always a step ahead of or behind the Los Angeles *Times* or the Federal Bureau of

Investigation. Often doors were opened only once. When we were there first we got cooperation. When we were second we got nothing."

How do you persuade the mother or father of a murderer, or the relative or friend of someone else who has achieved notoriety, to talk with you? Often such persons don't need to be persuaded. If they do need persuasion, one strong argument is that the interest of their friend or relative will be better served if the public knows the truth about him, as they see it, than if the press is forced to rely on scratchy information or pure speculation.

As I have indicated, however, ordinarily the best interviews are planned in advance. To get such an interview you must tell the person you want to interview who you are, with whom you're affiliated, what you want to talk about, how long the interview will take, and where it will be held.

Who you are is obvious enough. If you hold a high position in your organization, it's wise to make this plain. People who agree to be interviewed like to talk with someone who sounds important.

In telling what you want to talk about, be as specific as possible. Tell the person you approach not only the general subject you want to ask about but also, if possible, a few of the key questions you will pose. This should not only help you get the interview, but should also help the other party prepare to talk with you.

As a matter of fact, on occasion the other party may ask to see a list of questions you plan to ask, in advance of the interview. As a general rule, it's wise to cooperate with such a request. A more thoughtful interview may result.

If such a request is not made, you'll probably do as well not to offer to provide a list of questions in advance, unless you believe the interviewee will have to check his records in order to answer. After all, there's much to be said for obtaining a man or woman's spontaneous answers.

It's very important to make plain about how much time you'll want. Nothing can be more frustrating than to plan on a two-hour interview if the person you are interviewing has set aside only one hour. And this will often be the case with, say, a top business executive unless you have made plain your desires beforehand.

Just how much time should you ask for? There can be no flat answer to that question. Some reporters have conducted very successful interviews while taking a 10-minute taxicab ride with a governor or senator. Television reporters have sometimes been able to obtain significant statements in considerably less time than that.

Almost always, however, an interview of this length results in what is known as hard news—the kind of news that makes front-page newspaper stories. The newspaper or magazine reporter who must write a feature story obviously needs much more time.

Sometimes, in fact, an interview can run on for days. For example, an editor of *Playboy* once flew to Switzerland to interview John Kenneth Galbraith, the noted Harvard economist who served as ambassador to India. Galbraith was on a winter vacation in Gstaad, and the interview took up an hour or two of seven consecutive evenings.

Other reporters have been known to accompany celebrities for a day or even several days in order to get the kind of story they wanted. Obviously, to get this much time from anyone you must represent a very well-known organization, and you must ask for the interview quite smoothly.

The typical interview should not last less than one hour or more than two and one-half hours. Especially if you want to interview someone on a subject of some substance, be reluctant to accept less than an hour—and certainly not less than forty-five minutes. Otherwise you just will not have time to ask all the questions you need to ask. And you will run the risk that the person you interview will just be getting warmed up when time runs out.

On the other hand, people usually run out of steam after two or two and one-half hours of continuous talking. So try not to ask for more, at any one sitting. In recent years I twice interviewed men for four hours. I had prepared carefully in advance, and the interviews went well. But at the end, both the interviewees and I were exhausted.

Deciding on where you will hold an interview is rarely difficult. In the vast majority of cases it will be understood that you will go to the office, home, hotel room, or whatever of the person you want to interview. It is simply a matter of courtesy that you go to the person you want to interview rather than ask him to come to see you.

Occasionally he may want to reverse this procedure. This may be the case if he is visiting the city in which your publication, studio, or station is located.

Wherever the interview is held, privacy is imperative. If you are visiting the person you are interviewing, then you must depend on him or her to prevent undue interruptions. If he is visiting you, the burden of privacy is on you. Nothing can do more to throw an interview off course than frequent interruptions.

This chapter began with the obvious truth that the only way to get an interview is to ask for it. But it also included the suggestion that, in many, though far from all, cases it is wise to approach the person you want to interview through a third party.

The nation's great reporters, however, often take the bull by the horns. Even if they work through a third party, they may not hesitate to ask for an interview when no one else has asked before.

On Wednesday, February 15, 1950, a day that brought news of the signing of a 30-year alliance between Communist China and the Soviet Union, plus a plea by Winston Churchill for a top-level parley aimed at ending the atomic bomb race, the major story on the front page of the *New York Times* mentioned neither of these events. Rather, it was an exclusive interview that began:

"In the age of atomic energy, transmuted into a weapon which can destroy great cities and the best works of civilization, and in the shadow of a hydrogen detonant which could multiply many times that agent of destruction, a serene President of the United States sits in the White House with undiminished confidence in the triumph of humanity's better nature and the progress of his own efforts to achieve abiding peace.

"This President, Harry S Truman, is a controversial figure in the world and in domestic politics. But to those who talk with him intimately about the problem of global life and death, his faith that these good things will happen, and probably in his own time, shines out with a luminous and simple quality which no event or misadventure of policy can diminish."

The interview, of course, was with the thirty-third President of the United States. It covered many subjects—the so-called Cold War, deficit spending by the federal government, civil rights, and several others. It was conducted by Arthur Krock, then chief of the Washington Bureau of the *New York Times*. And it created an instant furor in the nation's capital.

A member of the House of Representatives went so far as to attach an amendment to a bill before Congress—an amendment that would have barred any President, any member of his Cabinet, or any head of a government department from granting exclusive interviews. Several members of the Washington press corps heatedly asked the President about the interview at his next press conference. And the President curtly told them to cool off.

It was true, of course, that Presidents rarely gave exclusive interviews. Woodrow Wilson had given a few. So had Truman himself—although never on such a broad scale or in the question-and-answer format that Krock had employed.

But these earlier interviews had definitely been exceptions. It had been a long-standing custom that, when a President spoke to the press, he spoke to all its members simultaneously. The press corps had come to rely on this custom, and it had been scooped.

As you can guess, the furor soon died down. Fifteen months later Krock was awarded a special mention by Columbia University in lieu of a Pulitzer Prize. The Pulitzer Prize advisory board made plain that he would have won the national reporting prize outright if he had not been a member of the advisory board and if it had not been the policy of the board not to give prizes to its own members. As it was, the committee did not give an award for national reporting that year, asserting that Krock's interview had been the "outstanding achievement" in the field.

As a matter of fact, Krock did not need another award. He had already won two Pulitzer Prizes for national reporting—one in 1935 and the other in 1938. Ironically, the second had also been for an exclusive interview—with President Franklin D. Roosevelt.

Did Krock obtain his exclusive interview with Harry S Truman because he was one of the most distinguished journalists in Washington? Unquestionably. Did he also obtain it because he was connected with the country's, and perhaps the world's, most distinguished newspaper? Almost certainly.

But is it not also true that there were at least a few other distinguished newspapers in the land, with at least a few outstanding journalists on their staffs? Is it not clear, then, that, whatever Krock's prestige and affiliation, he got his interview because he had asked for it when no one else thought to?

The lesson is plain: Enterprise has always paid off in journalism, and it always will. Go thou and do likewise.

4. *How to Prepare for an Interview*

If I could write only one chapter on the subject of interviewing, this would be that chapter. The reason is quite simple. Nothing is more important to the success of most interviews than advance preparation.

In some cases, of course, there is no opportunity to prepare in advance. Thus a newspaper reporter on general assignment may be hurriedly detailed to cover a major hotel fire. He will have no chance to check in advance on how many rooms the hotel has or on whether anyone of importance is staying there. Nor will he have time to prepare questions. He will have to work swiftly and surely after the fact, drawing on all his skills and experience so as to ask the right questions and ascertain the information he needs.

Even the newspaper reporter who specializes in some area like finance or state politics may not have much time to check on the background of a fast-breaking story or to formulate the most important questions to ask. He must draw on what knowledge he already has.

But the newspaperman who is writing a feature story, the magazine writer who is doing an article, the television reporter who is preparing a documentary, and the public relations executive who is ghostwriting a speech all have time to do their homework. Normally this homework can be broken into two parts—reading about the subject at hand and preparing questions to ask about it.

Very often the journalist is judged consciously or unconsciously—by his superiors and by his reading, listening, or viewing audience—on how well he does these two things. And he should be. For question asking can be an art in itself. As Voltaire said, "Judge a man by his questions rather than by his answers."

How should you prepare to ask questions? By first deciding what information you want to get. The more specific and clear-cut you can make your objectives the better off you will be.

For example, if you were assigned to interview a former President of the United States who had been out of office for ten years, several possibilities would present themselves. You could plan on doing a human interest story, concentrating on what the former President's hobbies were and how he was spending his retirement years. Or you could plan on asking him what he thought of his successors and their performance in office. Or you could ask his views about the nation or the world in general. Or you could ask his predictions for the future. Unless you were very lucky as to the amount of time you had been granted, you could not hope to cover all these possibilities adequately in a single interview.

Once you have decided the general subject you want to cover, you should make your goals even more specific, if at all possible. For example, in the case cited above, you might decide that, whatever else the interview covered, you must find out the former President's views on three tradition-breaking pieces of legislation recently enacted by the Congress.

Obviously, deciding on the nature of the interview you

want to hold requires that you know something about the man you want to interview. How much needs to be known varies greatly. Nonetheless, it is usually important to know something, for such knowledge may even affect the way you begin the interview.

Thus, a theater reporter for the *New York Times* has observed that conventional question-and-answer interviews will not always work—or at least work in full—with some of today's hippier young actors and actresses. Some of the actors just don't like the somewhat formal structure of a question-and-answer interview. As a result, some reporters now just browse around an actor's living room and wait for him to begin the interview by making some interesting observation. Or they make some wildly improbable remark in the hope that he will answer back.

It can often be quite easy to learn something about a man in advance of an interview. Has he written any books or articles or made any speeches about the subject you want to interview him about? If so, get hold of them. They can reduce by half both the time you need to prepare for the interview and the time you actually need for question asking. They can also help you ask better and more precise questions.

Is the man listed in *Who's Who*? Have any other publications published articles on him? Check the *Reader's Guide to Periodical Literature* and similar sources. The information you glean may not only provide answers to some questions you had planned to pose but also suggest more fruitful areas for inquiry.

If it's usually important to know something about the person you plan to interview, it's also wise to know something about the environment in which he works or operates. The Columbia Broadcasting System indicated just how important this can be during the 1968 presidential primaries.

It assigned its television reporters to cover geographical areas as well as candidates. Explained a CBS executive: "There are always two sides to a campaign—the candidate and the region he campaigns in. Each of our men is expected to know the history of the area he covers, its power sources and its issues, in order that he may accurately measure the impact of a candidate. A man who only follows a candidate can't do that."

If the person you want to interview is a businessman rather than a politician, then he may work for a publicly owned company. If so, it publishes an annual report for its stockholders. Get hold of the two most recent issues and read them. It won't be necessary to master them in every detail. But it will be wise to have a good idea of what product or service the company provides, of what its recent profit record is, and of what its future plans are. In fact, the annual report itself may suggest some questions. So, too, may other corporate publications, such as internal and external house organs.

If the person you want to interview is an actor, he may have appeared in several movies, television shows, or on-or-off-Broadway plays. Newspapers and magazines have probably commented on his performances and perhaps interviewed him at earlier stages of his career as well. Thus a great deal of information may be at your disposal prior to the interview.

If the person you want to interview is a sports star, a wealth of statistics has been compiled on his performance on the playing field. No doubt his athletic skills become apparent early in life. As a result, there may be interesting reports about him dating back to his high-school days.

It is often easy to get information like this in advance of an interview, sometimes not so easy. It is sometimes important to gather a great deal of such information, sometimes not so important. You can easily waste a great deal of time in research like this. In particular, you can read too carefully material that is not especially pertinent to the subject at hand.

How much time you should spend on advance research depends on how much time you have, how important the man you want to interview is, what the particular subject you want to interview him about is, how important the resulting article is expected to be, and other obviously related factors. In general, it is safe to say that you should spend as much time on this kind of research as you possibly can. But in so doing work swiftly. Gather a lot of information, but eliminate quickly anything that is not relevant, and devote your attention to the rest.

As you do this, jot down the questions that occur to you. This will save you the trouble of going over a second time all the material you have gathered.

Then compile your questions in a logical order. Some editors or writers like to go into interviews with only a few key questions written down or even with all their questions in their heads. If this method works for them, who is to quarrel with it?

I prefer a much more comprehensive approach. I type out all the questions I plan to ask, in the order I plan to ask them.

It seems to me that this method has several advantages. First, it ensures that I will remember all the points I wish to cover. Second, it makes it easier to keep the interview on track. For what inevitably happens, in nine interviews out of ten, is simple enough to describe. The interviewee answers the first five or six questions in order. But when he is asked the seventh question he somehow manages to answer the twenty-seventh instead.

Then the problem immediately arises: Does the interviewer go on to the twenty-eighth question or does he go back to the eighth? There can be no easy answer to this problem. But if the interviewer has all his questions written out, it is much easier to skip back and forth with the interviewee, as he wishes, and then lead him forward again in orderly fashion. In short, most interviews become somewhat unstructured as they progress, and a written list of questions gives the interviewer a structure he can return to whenever he feels it necessary.

There is yet a third—and more subtle—reason for typing out your questions. It is plain proof to the person you are interviewing that you have given some thought and trouble to preparing the interview. If this is not the sincerest form of flattery, it is the next thing to it. It is also a subtle suggestion to the interviewee that, if you have devoted some thought to the questions you will ask, he should give some thought to the answers he will give.

If you want still another reason for preparing an interview in advance, remember that, if you don't know precisely what you want to ask, there is always the danger that you will run out of questions. This can be very embarrassing indeed.

No doubt you remember Spencer Tracy, the famous actor who won two Oscars and the plaudits of millions of movie fans. As an actor he often portrayed strong and good men. It was hard not to love him.

Yet in private life he could be somewhat crusty. In fact, he guarded his privacy like a bulldog and was particularly adverse to giving interviews. On the few occasions when he did give them he proved very difficult to deal with.

One reporter found this out the hard way, when he made the mistake of asking Tracy what qualities make a woman attractive. The actor thought the question was silly, and he quickly rejoined, "Young man, I'll give you thirty seconds to think of another question." The reporter didn't have one ready, and he couldn't think of one off the top of his head. Whereupon the interview abruptly ended.

In preparing questions for an interview, remember to be careful of the way you phrase your questions. Public opinion pollsters have long known that the way questions are phrased can drastically affect the answers. As a result, they go to great pains to word their questions so as to avoid any show of partiality and so as to prevent people from feeling that they are expected to answer in a certain way. This kind of painstaking care can be very important, because some people are highly susceptible to influence.

The lesson is plain enough: Avoid asking leading questions. The less intelligent and educated the person you interview the more apt he will be to tell you what you want to hear—which may not be either the truth or his own real opinion. And the more intelligent and well educated the person the more apt he will be to see through your ploy— and to resent it.

Another lesson is: Be careful of what qualifying words you use. Words like "always," "never," "sometimes," "usually," "very," and so on can markedly affect the meaning of a question—and, of course, the answer you receive. You must use such words sometimes. In fact, it is often wise to use them. But use them with care and make sure the interviewee understands how they affect the meaning of a question.

It follows, of course, that another rule for preparing an interview is: Make sure your questions are very clear. In this connection, bear in mind that we almost all talk somewhat differently from the way we write. When we talk we are apt to be informal, to condense our statements, and to count on gestures to convey some of our meaning. So, if you draw up a list of written questions, remember that you will be tempted to phrase the questions just a little differently when you actually ask them.

There is a good way around this problem, however. When you write your questions down, pretend you are actually posing them to the person you are going to interview. With a little practice you will pick up the knack of rewriting and rephrasing the questions as you are apt to ask·them.

Another way to ensure that your questions are clear is to make them as specific as possible. This is not always feasible, of course. Sometimes it is not even wise. If, say, you are dealing with a truly brilliant man, it is sometimes best to ask broad, general questions, then let him carry the ball.

Nonetheless, as a general rule, specific questions beget specific answers. General questions beget general—and often useless—answers.

Still another way to ensure clarity is to avoid asking several questions at once. Ask one question at a time, even if you have to break what is naturally a several-part question into two or three questions. If you don't follow this procedure, you will often create confusion and receive disorganized answers.

If concrete, specific questions, asked one at a time, usually produce good interviews, bear in mind that this approach can be overdone. It can result in a sort of staccato interview, in which the interviewee answers accurately but much too briefly.

So be prepared to include some open-end questions, both to relieve the monotony of a long string of specific questions and to draw out the interviewee. Such questions often begin: What do you think about . . . ? Or, what sort of factors do you think . . . ? Or, what do you mean by . . . ? One internationally known management consulting firm has found that these kinds of questions often do the most to put the interviewee in a reflective, thoughtful mood.

Always be ready to ask basic, fundamental questions. As indicated earlier, it is important to do your homework and to know something about the subject at hand and about the person you will talk with. But unless you are a specialist, it is usually impossible to understand every facet of the subject at hand. So, unless you ask so many basic, elementary questions that the interviewee concludes that you are either an ignoramus or that you haven't done your homework, you cannot often go wrong by trying to clear up any points about his thinking or his profession that you don't understand. Most people who agree to be interviewed are willing to be helpful. Sometimes they are even pleased to assume the role of teacher.

There's another reason for being willing to ask basic questions. Sometimes you can obtain new and interesting insights into old problems. Thus I once had occasion to question several company presidents about the nature of leadership. Now, everyone knows what leadership is. But have you ever tried to define it—vividly and accurately and in only a few words? It's nowhere nearly so easy as you may think.

But two of the presidents got at the problem in a very interesting way—by telling me what leadership wasn't. As one of them put it: "Leadership is not mere drive. It is not merely the ability to get things done. Lots of men can get things done, but often these things have to be done their way and no one else's. As a result, they may be able to get a job done, but they may not be able to get other people to do it."

Take another example of the importance of being willing to ask basic questions—which, in some cases, may mean seeming to ask the obvious. As the story was related to me, a newly installed Secretary of State was holding his first press conference, and he was asked to comment on the basic purposes of the North Atlantic Treaty Organization. Whereupon he replied, briefly and rather testily, that the purposes of NATO were well known and that the new administration did not plan any changes in them.

When the conference was over, he exploded in private over the reporter's supposed stupidity and asked an aide who he was. Whereupon the aide was compelled to give him the name of one of the most famous newspapermen in the country. To top it all off, the next day the reporter's newspaper carried a front-page story to the effect that the new administration planned no major changes in our military and foreign policies in relation to Western Europe.

Remember that lesson: A truly great reporter is not afraid to appear stupid in order to get a worthwhile story.

One other bit of advice: Don't be afraid to ask tough questions, but don't ask dirty questions. By tough questions I mean questions that cause a man to think, to reflect, to search and, if necessary, to clear up any discrepancies in earlier statements he may have made on the same subject. To such questions you may not always get the kind of answers you seek. But if you ask six men the same tough question and five give you superficial answers, I think you will find that the sixth will often come through with a meaningful response.

But never ask dirty questions. By dirty questions I mean questions that are devoid of serious purpose and that are basically designed to embarrass the person you are interviewing—for no good reason. Dirty questions do no one any good, least of all the reputation of journalism. Besides, if you persist in asking them, sooner or later you will get your comeuppance.

Like the children of many famous men, those of Sir Winston Churchill had their problems and their ups and downs. As Randolph Spencer Churchill, Winston's only son, once put it, "When it is living under the shadow of a great oak tree, the sapling, so close to the parent tree, does not perhaps receive enough sunshine."

And yet Randolph Churchill apparently inherited enough of his father's flashing, devastating wit to put down any journalist. Once, while he was in this country, a television reporter asked him about his sister, Sarah, who had been arrested and fined for being drunk in public.

Snapped the younger Churchill: "I wouldn't think of asking you about your sisters. I was warned. They said, 'Don't you trust them. They'll spring something dirty, mean or caddish on you.' I've not been disappointed—"

"Who told you not to trust us?" the television interviewer interrupted.

"I never reveal my sources of information," Churchill retorted. "I'm a journalist, not a television interviewer. I don't bother to look up what your sister has done or who your father was. I don't even know if you had a father or if you know who your father was."

If it's important to choose and phrase your questions with care, it's also important to present them in an organized manner. In listing your first few questions, bear two thoughts in mind. Don't start so slowly that your interviewee will quickly become bored. But at the same time start slowly enough—that is, in a sufficiently neutral vein—so that you don't intimidate him or give him the feeling that he can't cope with you. Thus your first three or four questions should usually be fairly easy to answer. Wait until the fourth or fifth before you begin to bore in on the subject at hand.

As for the rest of your questions, it should be easy enough to present them in good order. Just remember that the interview should move forward from one logical point to the next. The interviewee, to be sure, will probably jump about a bit. If so, you can more easily pick up the threads if your questions have been put into some logical pattern.

By organizing you can save both your own time and that of the person you are interviewing. And, as is the case with so many other things in life, how you use interviewing time can be all-important.

In writing this chapter I have made two assumptions. The first is that you know when to interview and when not to interview. The second is that you will pick your inter- viewees with care. A word or two about both assumptions may be in order.

In general, the interview is most useful when it is em- ployed to obtain opinions—and opinions on matters of some significance. It is much less useful when it is used primarily or exclusively to obtain factual information.

There are two reasons for this. One, the written record is a more reliable source of factual information than the human tongue. People often forget names, titles, figures, percentages, and all of the other precise data that can do so much to make an article or story or documentary seem— and be—well researched and factually accurate. What's more, although they may sometimes seem to remember such data, their memories may actually be in error. This can lead you into error yourself or cause you to undertake time-consuming cross-checking. Two, people will quickly become bored if most of your questions deal only with facts, and not with what they think about the facts. As a result, it's safe to say that you should never resort to an interview when you can get the needed information more quickly, more easily, and more reliably from a nonhuman source.

So far as picking interviewees with care goes, have some reason for approaching a man or woman for an interview. That reason can only be that there is some evidence that he or she can comment authoritatively on the subject you are investigating.

But picking interviewees with care means even more. It means knowing when to interview just one person and when to interview several—or many.

Occasionally this question can only be decided after you have completed one or two interviews. Perhaps the persons you have interviewed have not given you as much information as you had hoped and you decide you must go elsewhere.

But it is usually best to decide on your number of interviewees in advance. You can go a long way toward making this decision by asking yourself two questions: First, how important is the first person you plan to interview? Is he so big, so famous, so in command of his field that his opinions in themselves are likely to form the basis for a solid story? Second, how broad is the subject you want to write about? Is it so broad, so subject to different approaches and different opinions, that no one man can be expected to have the final word on it or anything resembling the final word?

The answer to this latter question will sometimes be obvious. In other cases, answering it will require all the journalistic experience and intuition you can master.

5. *How to Record an Interview*

Twenty-five years ago this chapter wouldn't have been written. Or, if it had been written, it would have been written differently. That's because there was really only one way to record an interview. That one way consisted of putting notes down on paper with pen or pencil.

Today this is no longer the case. Within recent years the portable tape recorder has made many recruits among journalists in all media. I do not know how many of them use tape recorders on a regular, as opposed to an occasional, basis, and I doubt that any figures are available. I would imagine, however, that such reporters are still in a very decided minority.

Even so, the tape recorder has made a splash. It's shown up at news conferences held by candidates for the United States Presidency and at interviews conducted with servicemen in bunkers in Vietnam. The Columbia University Graduate School of Journalism, the bellwether of America's journalism schools, now requires its students to gain some experience with the recorders. And at least one magazine editor says he considers his portable tape recorder as essential a part of his equipment as his typewriter.

In fact, the tape recorder has done more than make a

splash. In some cases it has enabled the talented, intelligent nonjournalist to compete on equal terms with the professional journalist.

Just a few years ago, for example, a professor of economics and finance at New York University's Graduate School of Business Administration traveled 75,000 miles throughout the United States and Canada, taping interviews with men who had played major league baseball during the first twenty years of this century. He let them reminisce not only about themselves but also about Ty Cobb, Christy Mathewson, and the other great stars of their era.

Then he wrote a book in which he recorded their memories almost exactly as they had spoken them into his tape recorder. The book was called *The Glory of Their Times,* and it was unquestionably a masterpiece of its kind. In fact, one big city newspaper called it the best book ever written on baseball "any time, for any reason."

The many advantages of the portable tape recorder make it necessary to ask the question: Should the wise journalist use it, on a regular basis, instead of paper and pencil? Before discussing that question, I had better make three of my own biases plain:

First, I am a paper-and-pencil man. I have used the tape recorder in the past—rarely. I will use it in the future—rarely. By and large I will stick to note-taking.

Second, this does not mean that paper and pencil are inherently superior to the tape recorder. It merely means that they work best for me. For other journalists the opposite is true.

This is an important point. For the question is not how a journalist gets his stories, provided he gets them intelligently and ethically. The question is whether he gets them at all. In short, the wise journalist will use the tool that suits him best—and let the competition be damned.

Finally, whatever tool he uses on a regular basis, the good journalist will have a sound working knowledge of both paper and pencil and the tape recorder. He will be able both to take good notes and to use a recorder—and be able to do so on short notice. The reason is that there are situations in which one tool is inherently superior to the other or even in which one must be used rather than the other.

For example, a member of the Washington press corps must know how to take notes, if for no other reason than that tape recorders are not permitted at the so-called background conferences sometimes held by the President, Cabinet officers, or other key officials of the federal government. Reporters who attend these conferences, which sometimes provide a great deal of useful information, are not allowed to attribute this information to the official who gives it but must credit it to "a high State Department official" or to "parties close to the President" or to some other unspecific source. Sometimes, in fact, the reporters are not allowed to attribute the information to anyone. It must seem to come from themselves and their general knowledge of the nation's political situation.

Obviously, a tape recorder is not allowed at "backgrounders," because the officials who give them want to minimize the risk that their identities will be leaked—and proved. Reporters who attend these conferences observe the ground rules on pain of having their sources of information dry up in the future should they not observe them.

There are other situations where a tape recorder would not be welcome. Some people don't mind being quoted but don't want to be quoted quite so precisely as a tape recorder would allow. Other people—among them Norman Mailer, the novelist—complain that tape recorders destroy the mood and the intimacy that can build up between a journalist and the person he is interviewing. Still others don't like what the tape recorder reveals about their ability to handle the English language.

I know of one company president who violently opposed use of a tape recorder in an upcoming interview. He had seen the transcript of an earlier tape-recorded interview he had given, and he had decided that his spoken use of the English language was not exactly eloquent.

Actually, the man was intelligent and well educated and had a good deal to say. But anyone who has ever read a few transcripts of tape-recorded interviews can sympathize with his viewpoint. In speaking the English language most of us get our syntax garbled, employ a few non sequiturs, fail to answer questions concisely and neatly, and in general reveal that we all write English better than we speak it.

Take the other side of the coin. There are instances in which tape recorders are, if not mandatory, almost so. This might well be the case if a journalist were about to write a biography of some living person or ghost an autobiography. In many such cases the journalist might interview the person involved for 20, 30, 50, possibly 100 or more hours— in, of course, suitable segments. And generally speaking, a journalist who interviews one person for 50 hours will do better to use a recorder than depend on his notes. When there is that much information to take down, the recorder will do a more thorough job than the human hand.

There are other instances in which a tape recorder can prove invaluable. If a reporter covers a conference where two or more speeches will be given simultaneously and where copies of these speeches will not be available, he can cover one speech in person and record another. Again, I have known rare instances in which people have said that they did not have time to grant a personal interview, but have told the reporters involved that, if the questions were forwarded by mail, they would tape their answers and mail the tape to the reporters.

Still and all, the typical journalist is not going to use a tape recorder two times out of three or paper and pencil two times out of three. He is going to use one tool or the other almost all of the time. So let's return to the original question—which tool should it be?—and look first at the advantages and disadvantages of the recorder.

The biggest advantage should be self-evident. The machine records—or should record—everything. This even the best of reporters, working with pencil and paper, cannot do. They can and should be able to record most things, especially all the main ideas of the persons they talk to. They may even capture *almost* everything. But unless an interview is very short and the person interviewed speaks very slowly, it is almost literally impossible for a reporter to take down every little word.

To this, of course, the experienced journalist may reply that it is rarely necessary to get down every little word. There are lots of words that aren't that important. And yet there are cases when it is desirable to do just that.

This might well be true if an interviewee were providing a journalist with a great deal of hard-to-understand technical material. It might also be true if an interviewee were to speak with a great deal of color or flavor, in a style all his own.

A couple of years ago, for instance, while holding an impromptu press conference, a Southern governor broke into a tirade against the federal government. Although the reporters present got down what he said, only one got it on tape. Yet when the governor had finished, all the other reporters turned to the man with the tape. "It wasn't so important what the governor said," the reporter later explained, "but how he said it—the rhythm, the lack of structure."

All this is not to say that you should automatically turn to a tape recorder if you are going to interview someone known to speak colorfully. After all, Casey Stengel, the former manager of the New York Yankees and then the New York Mets, for years spoke to sportswriters in a lively, colorful, garbled kind of verbal shorthand that could have driven the uninitiated up the walls. Yet many of these sportswriters got all—or enough—of Stengel's words down on paper so as to bring baseball's grand old man across clearly and interestingly to readers of newspaper sports pages. It is to say, however, that, if you are going to interview someone who speaks colorfully, you might at least consider using a recorder.

You might do the same if you know you will be interviewing someone who is known to speak very rapidly. Governor Ronald Reagan of California does this, and some reporters who do not ordinarily use tape recorders have taken to doing so with him in order to make sure that they don't miss anything important that he might say.

A tape recorder can also protect journalists against charges that they have misquoted the person or persons they interviewed. In a mayoralty campaign in Boston not long ago the reporters on one newspaper finally decided that they had to use tape recorders because one of the candidates kept charging that her views were being misreported. With tapes the reporters were able to prove exactly what she had said.

In short, for a variety of reasons, it is sometimes good to have on tape a record of everything that was said. Yet the tape recorder offers other advantages or potential advantages as well. Some editors and reporters say that it enables them to relax and concentrate entirely on what they are asking and how an interviewee is responding, without having to worry about taking notes. Others say that a tape recorder can be particularly useful if they must interview a political candidate or anyone else in the midst of a noisy crowd. That's because they don't have to shove and push their way forward so that they are immediately adjacent to or in front of the man they are interviewing. They can be one or two men away from him and simply hold their microphones out. Often the microphones will pick up what the reporters can't hear.

There's one advantage of the tape recorder that is rarely mentioned—and perhaps rarely thought of. The recorder can enable a journalist not only to rehear the persons he interviews but also to rehear himself. This can be more important than you may think.

To some extent the success of an interview depends upon the rapport the interviewer establishes with an interviewee. And by playing back a few tape-recorded interviews a journalist can learn a great deal about himself and the way he asks questions. He can learn in particular about his tone of voice. This is worth knowing, because often the tone in which a question is asked affects the answer that is given more than the question itself.

The reporter can also learn how well he phrases his questions—in particular, how his spoken phrasing of them compares with the way he has written them out in advance. He can find out how often he interrupts—and how he does so. He can find out if he is dominating interviews or if he is letting opportunities to ask questions pass by. In short, by playing back several tape-recorded interviews and by studying his style of interviewing a journalist may do much to make himself a better one.

Before turning to the disadvantages of the tape recorder,

there's one other point worth noting. Tape recorders are no longer the heavy, bulky, cumbersome pieces of equipment that they once were. Many are now light, compact, and easy to carry. For example, the so-called cassette tape recorders now weigh four pounds or less and can easily be slung over one's shoulder.

What's more, the cassettes now provide for two hours' worth of recording. This means that the interviewer can let the recorder run for one hour before touching it.

To top it all off, the cassettes are not particularly expensive. Most of them range in price from $50 to $100, and there is a sizable number to choose from.

All this is not to say that there are not other good portable tape recorders on the market. But one editor I know of with a particularly good working knowledge of tape recorders recommends the cassettes because of their portability, their good performance, and their general ease of use.

The greatest advantage of the tape recorder—its ability to record everything—is also its greatest disadvantage. That's because transcribing from a tape recorder takes a lot of time—more than many editorial offices can spare on a sustained basis. In fact, even listening to a tape takes a lot of time. Harrison Salisbury, an assistant managing editor of the *New York Times* with a Pulitzer Prize to his credit, says: "I rarely use the tape recorder, simply for mechanical reasons. You have to play the damn thing through, and that's like holding two interviews. I don't have that much time."

I know of any number of other editors and writers who don't use tape recorders, on a regular basis at least, for the very same reason. In the end this may well be the main reason why the tape recorder will never really supplant paper and pencil.

The tape recorder is also liable to pick up foreign sounds,

and this can make it difficult for the interviewer or a secretary to hear what was said when the tape is played back. Air-conditioning machines can be particularly intrusive. So can the sound of a man tapping his fingernails on a table while he speaks.

In addition, tape recorders often do not work well in a group interview. That's because the participants sometimes have a tendency to speak all at the same time, and this makes it virtually impossible for the transcriber to know what was said or who said it.

Finally, there's the simple fact that tape recorders sometimes just don't work. Often the fault is human. Perhaps the interviewer forgets to turn the machine on or makes some other silly error that prevents it from recording. In other cases the error is not human. The machine or the tape breaks down.

I had this happen once in an interview with a personnel executive in New York—and didn't know it. When I got back to the office and found that the interview hadn't been recorded, I rechecked the tape. I found that it had been torn during an interview held by another editor and subsequently spliced together with Scotch Tape. The machine had stopped recording the minute it had reached the Scotch Tape.

The possibility that a tape recorder will not record is worth remembering. There is hardly an editor or reporter of my acquaintance who has not suffered at least one fiasco with a tape recorder—and usually a total fiasco. Sometimes the editors have been embarrassed at their own oversights, sometimes outraged at the breakdown of the machine. In fact, I know of some journalists who are so aware of and wary of machine failure that they always protect themselves by taking rough notes. To which the obvious comment is:

If you think you must take notes, why use a tape recorder in the first place?

If journalists are outraged when a tape recorder fails to work, you can imagine how the people they have interviewed have sometimes felt. One of the worst cases I have heard about involved a very well-known U.S. senator. He was once interviewed for approximately two hours. Through an oversight on the part of the interviewer, the tape recorder failed to pick up a single word.

The interview was an important one. So the interviewer had to go back to the senator, confess what had happened, and ask for another chance. Almost needless to say, the senator was furious. The embarrassed editor got what he asked for, but the interview did not last anything like two hours. It lasted about thirty minutes.

All of which brings up the advantages and disadvantages of note-taking. They can be more easily recounted.

The biggest advantage of paper and pencil is speed. Not speed of recording. The tape recorder can record more rapidly than the moving pencil and to varying degrees, depending on the skill of the journalist, somewhat more thoroughly, too. Nor does paper and pencil's advantage in speed involve just the fact that a reporter can work immediately from notes, whereas, if he uses a tape, he will have to wait for a transcript or else listen to a playback of his tape.

Paper and pencil boast another advantage involving speed. This rests in the fact that a reporter who has taken ten pages of notes is in a much better position to go to work than a reporter who must work from thirty to forty pages of transcript. Any journalist who has ever worked from a transcript and who has had to wade back and forth among the pages to find what was important—all the time disregarding digressions, non sequiturs, and the like—can attest to this fact. To put the matter in a single sentence, it is much easier and swifter to write a story from notes than it is to write it from a transcript—counting from the time the transcript is ready.

In journalism speed is almost always important, sometimes all-important. So the journalist pondering how to handle a particular assignment must always give this factor weight. Often the weight will go against the tape recorder.

As already indicated, there are instances in which the tape recorder, if not banned outright, will not be welcome. It is rare indeed for a man to agree to be interviewed, then balk at having notes taken, unless he has so specified in advance. He may ask that certain individual remarks be kept confidential, but he is not apt to object to note-taking in general. But if a man agrees to be interviewed and finds that the interview will be tape recorded, he may agree to this only very reluctantly. Sometimes he will balk for reasons already indicated—e.g., an awareness that spoken words rarely read as well as written words—sometimes for other reasons.

Whatever the reason, when a man agrees only reluctantly to have an interview recorded, the whole course of the interview is likely to be affected. He may not give out information that he would have given out if the reporter had only taken notes. Or he may speak in a much more guarded manner, with the result that the reporter will obtain less than a true reflection of the man. In short, the interviewee who dislikes or is unfamiliar with tape recorders may not give as good an interview as would otherwise be the case.

This doesn't mean, of course, that there are not people who do like to have interviews taped. There are indeed such people. Some, in fact, are unduly flattered to have their remarks recorded. Nonetheless, there are many who feel just the opposite.

All this is a long way of saying that note-taking is almost universally accepted in interviewing, while tape recording isn't. And the journalist who insists on using the recorder when it is not welcome may end up shortchanging himself and the organization he represents.

I'm sure that there are reporters whose pencil points have broken during interviews and who have had to take a moment out to borrow replacements from the persons they were interviewing. I'm sure there are reporters who have returned to their offices, only to find it difficult to decipher their own notes. I'm even sure there are reporters who have lost their notes (although I have never heard of any). Generally speaking, however, paper and pencil do not pose the problem of breakdown, through either human or mechanical failure, that the tape recorder does.

Finally, of course, paper and pencil are cheaper than the tape recorder. For a free-lance journalist, this advantage may be worth consideration. For the journalist employed by a magazine or a broadcasting system, however, it should not be a consideration—at least so far as the cost of the equipment goes. Even the smallest organization should be able to afford at least one tape recorder.

Yet the question of cost goes beyond the cost of the equipment. The time it takes a secretary to transcribe an interview can be very expensive, especially if such transcription takes place frequently. For just this reason one publication I know of allows—even encourages—its staff members to use tape recorders, but does not allow them to have the tapes transcribed. The editors must listen to the tapes themselves and, ironically, are often forced to take notes while the tapes are played back.

The major disadvantage of note-taking, of course, is that it can rarely record everything. And, as I've already indicated, there are occasions when it is important that just about everything be recorded. As a general rule, however, there is much to be said for the quick jibe of an old Associated Press reporter, "If you can't trust your notes in this game, then you'd better get out of it."

Note-taking is a part of journalism and almost certainly always will be. And the journalist who regularly uses a tape recorder because he thinks it can do a vastly better job of recording a conversation than he can is skating on very thin professional ice.

The assertion of some journalists that the tape recorder allows them to concentrate on asking questions and listening to answers without worrying about taking notes has merit. Interviewing with paper and pencil for any extended period of time does require intense concentration. The interviewer must ask questions, listen to answers, and take notes. He must also be alert to the necessity of probing into matters for which he has not prepared but which the interview itself makes plain must be looked into.

In short, interviewing by note-taking is hard work, requiring total alertness. But if a journalist knows his subject, has prepared for the interview in advance, and has mastered the art of note-taking, it is not as hard as all that. And it is something that any journalist is going to have to do many times in his career, no matter how often he uses a tape recorder.

To repeat what was said earlier, the wise journalist will know how both to take notes and to use a tape recorder. But for the journalist who prefers to use a recorder most of the time here are a few simple tips toward its more effective use:

First, know your machine. Know how it works. Know what it will do and know what it will not do. To begin to gain mastery over the machine, study its instruction manual thoroughly. Then practice with the machine for a while in the confines of your own office. Knowing your machine will not only enable you to get the most out of it but will also greatly reduce the chances that it will fail to record through an error or oversight on your part.

Second, whenever you are planning to use a recorder, take along more tape than you expect to use. The interview may turn out to be longer and more important than you had anticipated. How much more tape you should take along will depend on your circumstances, but possibly it should be twice as much as you think you will use.

Third, ask permission to tape record interviews. It isn't necessary to ask permission to take notes. But, for reasons given earlier, it is wise to ask if it's all right to record. If you run into a balky interviewee, tell him that you'll be glad to shut the machine off any time he wants to say something in confidence. Depending somewhat on the policies of the organization you work for, you may also be able to tell him that he will be given a chance to review the results of the interview prior to publication. And if it's true, of course, you can also tell him that you are not seeking sensational material nor trying to embarrass him or anyone else in any way.

Fourth, test your machine before the interview begins—and at least once during the course of the interview itself. If you have time and opportunity to do the checking before the interviewee actually comes into the room, so much the better. If not, just turn the machine on and ask him to give his name, title, and affiliation. Then let him listen to the playback. Getting him interested in the mechanics of the machine is one way of relaxing him and establishing rapport.

Fifth, turn the machine off after you have tested it. Don't turn it back on until the man starts answering your questions or says something important. Interview transcripts or playbacks take long enough without burdening them with the preliminary remarks with which most such conversations usually begin.

Finally, never hesitate to turn off the machine if the interviewee begins to digress. One editor I know says he gets around the apparent insult by saying: "Excuse me. I am interested in what you are saying. But I have a limited amount of tape, and I am going to cut the machine off for a moment." He swears the technique works—and often brings the interviewee back on course.

Also, of course, don't hesitate to turn the machine off if the interviewee receives a telephone call or someone steps into his office or living room.

What about the journalist who prefers note-taking? Here, advice is harder to give. For one thing, many journalists have evolved their own self-oriented techniques for taking notes. For another, I know from experience that they rarely think to exchange advice with their colleagues on this matter. Nevertheless, here are a few simple pointers:

First, learn how to abbreviate.

The reporters who are best equipped to take notes are those who have learned shorthand. But reporters like these are few and far between. I myself, in years past, once or twice considered taking a course in so-called Speedwriting, which I gather is a sort of poor man's shorthand. I never got around to doing so, but such courses may well have considerable value.

Without such a background, the good interviewer soon learns to develop his own informal shorthand. I have and, curious as it may sound, some of it varies from interview to interview, depending on the situation and my needs.

For example, I once had occasion to write an article on mutual funds, pension funds, and all the rest of the nation's so-called institutional investors. In order to write the article I had to interview several investment experts, and I knew in advance that they would all use the term "institutional investors" quite frequently. It's a big term to write out. So, in taking notes, I quickly abbreviated it to "ii."

There are all kinds of other possibilities. "Ind" can stand for "industry," "bus" for "business," and "gov" for the federal government. But these are only suggestions, and any journalist with a little imagination can work out the abbreviations that work best for him. He will need something along this order at some time or another—and usually many times—during the course of his career.

Second, learn to remember.

Any competent journalist gets down the high points of an interview. But often there is a great deal to write down—at great speed. So one thing I have learned to do is to listen so intently that I can remember whole anecdotes or vivid phrases for at least an hour or two afterwards. When the interview is over, I write down these anecdotes or phrases.

This is a good way to supplement note-taking, especially when an interviewee is pouring out information or opinions very quickly. Experience leads me to believe, however, that a journalist must use this device sparingly and that he cannot plan its use in advance.

When he can use it depends largely on the person he is interviewing. Usually it's when a person speaks very forcefully, colorfully, and vividly—when, in other words, a person would normally be apt to remember precisely what was said, even if he were not holding an interview.

Third, keep your pencil moving.

In almost every interview there come moments when the interviewee says things of little interest and moment. At such moments it is only natural to be tempted to stop writing.

Never stop for long. The typical interviewee is apt to feel pleased that you have sought out his opinions. He is also apt to feel a little puzzled and perhaps slightly affronted if he notices that you are no longer writing his opinions down. And notice he almost certainly will.

If he does, his enthusiasm for the interview may begin to die. To avoid this happening, keep your pencil moving most of the time, even if you only scribble. He will never know the difference.

Fourth, don't worry about brief lulls in your question-asking.

If an interviewee has anything at all of importance to say, he will sometimes get ahead of you. No matter how rapidly you write or how well you listen, you will still be taking notes when he has finished making a point. As a result, there will be a lull in the conversation before you ask your next question.

Unless these lulls are very frequent or last more than fifteen or twenty seconds, don't let them worry you or throw you off your pace. The interviewee will usually be flattered that you are taking notes so assiduously. More important, a few lulls will give him time to collect his thoughts and perhaps add comments he otherwise wouldn't have thought of. In fact, once in a while I find that some of an interviewee's most pointed remarks come just at the end of such a brief lull, after he has had a moment to reflect on what he has just said.

Fifth, review your notes as soon after an interview as possible.

On this point all the journalists I've ever talked with

about note-taking seem to agree. None of them put off the job of going over what they have written down.

If you can go over your notes almost immediately after an interview, so much the better. The conversation will still be fresh in your mind, and you can quickly fill in any gaps in your notes and write down anything tucked away in your memory. If you can't go over your notes at once, do so the same day or night. At the very outside, never delay beyond the following day. The human memory is more fallible than any of us like to think.

Sixth, don't depend on notes for long-term projects.

If you are going to use your notes the same day you take them, or the next day, or the next week, or within a month, fine. Especially if you take care to review the notes shortly after your interview, you should have no particular difficulty in transforming them into an article.

But if you are working on a long-term project and will be holding interviews over a period of many months, beware of relying on notes. Even if you review them shortly after an interview, you may find that, when you go to use them three or four months later, you will be somewhat at a loss. Words, phrases, figures, and anecdotes that might have seemed clear enough three or four days after an interview may not seem so clear now. In short, your interview may have diminished in value because you have forgotten most of the things your notes don't show and because the notes themselves, by their very nature, will not seem so clear.

I know of several journalists to whom this has happened. It happened to me once, too. Never again. I use my notes within a month of the time I take them—preferably sooner.

The moral would seem plain enough: If you don't think you will be getting at your notes soon, use a tape recorder. Or else, working from your notes, dictate a very detailed memo to yourself as soon after your interview as you can.

To sum up this chapter: In recording an interview, use the tool—tape recorder or pencil—that works best for you. But know how to use both. You never know when it will be wise—or necessary—to employ the tool you don't habitually rely on.

6. *How to Conduct an Interview*

Not long ago a press release from an internationally known management consulting firm crossed my
desk. The release dealt with a study the firm had made of
interviewing and question asking. Among other things, it
said that the success of an interview—any kind of interview—is determined during its first minute.

From time to time some preposterous statements are
made on interviewing. But this is one of the most preposterous ever written. If it were true, I wonder how any of us
would have enough courage to be interviewed for a new
job, to ask for the hand of a woman in marriage, or to
query a U.S. senator on his views on foreign policy. If it
were true, we'd spend too much time worrying if our ties
were straight enough, our smiles broad enough, and our
voices pleasant enough.

To be sure, it is incumbent upon an interviewer to do all
that he reasonably can to set an interviewee at ease at the
start of an interview. Basically, this means being pleasant
and friendly.

But to say that the success or failure of an interview is
determined in its first minute is little different from saying
that the outcome of a football game is determined in its first

minute. Occasionally one is, of course—perhaps because
the kickoff is run back for a touchdown and the opposing
team is demoralized. But games like this are the exception.
And so are interviews.

In fact, one rule for conducting successful interviews is
not to dawdle over opening pleasantries. Although it is important to be reasonably cordial, it is also important not to
waste much time on preliminary remarks, unless you expect
to see the person you are interviewing a number of times.
Often people are very busy and have taken time out of
overloaded schedules to be interviewed. They may resent it
if you seem to begin the interview by engaging in idle chit-
chat.

One of the best ways to begin an interview is to remind
the interviewee—very quickly—of the main subject of the
interview and of the ground you want to cover. If he is the
only person you plan to see, say so. He will attach more
importance to the interview. If you plan to see other people
as well, tell him so and tell him why further interviewing
will be necessary. Then begin with a few interesting but low-
key questions.

If it is important not to dawdle at the beginning of an
interview, it is also important not to dawdle during the
course of it. The typical interview lasts only an hour or two,
and none of this time should be wasted. Besides, if you
dawdle you run the risk that you will lose control of the
interview or that it will lack direction.

An earlier chapter indicated that it can be important for
an interviewer not to be afraid to ask basic questions—even
to appear uninformed if the occasion demands it. It is also
important for the interviewer not to try to be too clever. It
almost goes without saying, of course, that he should pose
intelligent, searching queries. But he should be straight-

forward about it and, unless circumstances are exceptional, avoid any attempt to put the interviewee on the defensive. Surreptitious attempts to pry information out of an interviewee or roundabout questioning are usually self-defeating. People respond to frankness and sincerity. They are on their guard when faced with someone who seems tricky or prone to show off his own knowledge.

As a matter of fact, of course, you will spend most of the time in an interview listening. Indeed, this is one of the most important things to know how to do—especially if you are taking notes at the same time. To do it well requires intense concentration.

Actually the art of listening requires even more. If you would be really successful as an interviewer, you must learn to listen with the inner ear. You must hear more than the words the interviewee speaks. You must catch his hidden feelings, his unexpressed reactions.

In many ways this kind of listening is really watching. For you must observe the nods of the head, the winks of the eye, and the gestures of the hand that often tell more about the interviewee's true reactions than what he is saying.

As one student of interviews puts it: "You must get at what a man means, not just what he says. Much relevant information is communicated in a most oblique way. You must get at the 'hows' and 'whys' in order to reach your objectives. Probing is the key skill in interviewing. And in probing you may have to evaluate the degree of the interviewee's personal experience in relation to what he is saying."

How can you best probe? Ask open-end questions: What do you think about . . . ? Ask reflective questions: Can you tell me a bit more about how you feel . . . ? Ask interpretive or summary questions: You're saying then that . . . ? Or ask problem questions: Let's suppose that you're president of a company faced with the following situation . . . ?

Careful listening is important for another reason. No matter how carefully you prepare for an interview, questions will occur to you during its course that didn't occur beforehand. It is very important that you ask these questions at the time they occur, for they may affect the whole course of the interview.

Be especially alert to ask about anything you don't understand or that seems questionable. I know of more than one editor or writer who has been called out on strikes because he has let such opportunities pass by or because he has allowed an interviewee to slip a curve ball past him without swinging at it.

A few years ago, for example, a young editor I know was assigned to interview some businessmen who had entered politics. His task was to get their opinions on the advisability of other businessmen following their lead.

Although none of the men he interviewed was as well known as, say, Governor Nelson Rockefeller of New York, one had been a governor of a small New England state and another had been a candidate for governor of one of the major states on the eastern seaboard. In short, the men the young editor interviewed were important men who knew what they were talking about.

He was scheduled to talk with six or eight such men, and his interviews were expected to extend over a period of several weeks. After a while a senior editor wanted to know how the younger man was doing. So he asked about the major disadvantages of businessmen going into politics. Without hesitation, the young editor replied, "The men I've talked with say there aren't any."

It was a ridiculous and revealing answer. For obviously a whole series of disadvantages would quickly come to almost anyone's mind. The cost of campaigning is one. The time campaigning takes is another. The possibility of being defeated is a third.

Despite these and other possibilities, the young editor had raised no objection when the men he interviewed said there were no disadvantages to a businessman's entering politics—presuming, of course, that he had asked about the disadvantages at all. I need hardly add, of course, that, because of these and other omissions, his article never quite came off.

More than once this book has emphasized the importance of being willing to ask tough questions, whether you have prepared them in advance or whether you must ask them on the spur of the moment. Nowhere was this need better illustrated than in a book that appeared a few years ago entitled *A Gift of Prophecy*.

As you may know, the book was about one Jeane Dixon, a Washington, D.C., housewife who is a so-called clairvoyant and who apparently has an amazing ability to predict what will happen in the future. For example, she apparently predicted the assassination of John F. Kennedy several years before he was even elected President.

A Gift of Prophecy was written by an experienced Washington political columnist named Ruth Montgomery, and it was both highly readable and highly interesting. Yet there was obviously something just a shade wrong with it. Perhaps it would be unfair to say that its attitude toward Mrs. Dixon was too adulatory. Nonetheless, without quite coming right out and saying so, it left the definite impression that Mrs. Dixon rarely erred in her predictions. This, despite the fact that she had erroneously predicted that World

War III would break out in 1958; that Red China would be admitted to the United Nations in 1959; and that Charles de Gaulle would surrender his power as leader of France in 1964.

It was left to a well-known male magazine writer, Bill Davidson, writing in the *Ladies' Home Journal* some months later, to get at the truth of the matter. It was he who asked the tough questions: How often do Mrs. Dixon's predictions fail to come true? And when that happens, why don't they come true?

His examination of the lady's published predictions over a 12-year period indicated that only about 60 percent of them had proved accurate. Interviews with her friends indicated that, when her predictions failed to come true, it was usually for one of two reasons: Either she had misinterpreted the symbols through which her foreknowledge comes. Or else the people about whom she had made predictions had changed their plans.

When you ask questions—especially tough questions—it can be important to check the answers that you receive. And this does not just mean checking factual answers with some outside source.

It can also mean checking the remarks of the person who is speaking to make sure you understand what he has meant. Probably the best way to do this is to repeat in your own words the gist of his remarks, then ask him if that is what he had in mind.

Checking the remarks of the person you are interviewing can also mean checking his authority to make them. Polltakers are prone to do this, and it is good that they do. For example, they may use what they call filter questions to ascertain an interviewee's knowledge of the subject at hand. Thus, if a polltaker is asking an interviewee about certain political matters, he may drop in some such question as: Do you happen to know the names of the two senators from your state?

Prepare in advance of the interview. Don't dawdle in getting started or in carrying through. Don't try to be too clever. Learn how to listen with more than common listening power. Don't let opportunities to ask key questions pass by. And don't fail to ask tough questions. All these are good rules for an interviewer to follow. But there is at least one other that is all-important: Never, never lose control of an interview.

An interview can go off the track for any one of several reasons. You may not have prepared in advance and may have no clear-cut purpose in mind. You may bore the interviewee by asking superficial, trivial questions. You may be up against an exuberant, dynamic personality who tends to seize control of things and talk only about those matters he wants to talk about. Or either you or the interviewee may get lost in some interesting but irrelevant digression.

It's usually easy enough to recognize when you've lost control of an interview. Either the interviewee is talking so much that you don't have a chance to ask questions. Or, if you are asking questions, you're not getting the kind of answers you want and need.

Actually, failure to maintain control of an interview is not, to the best of my knowledge, a common problem. But it can crop up when you least want it to do so. And the worst of it is, the man with whom it's most likely to crop up may be one of your best subjects. This is the man who may have set aside a lot of time for the interview, who may be highly and visibly enthusiastic about his work, and who may be only too delighted to tell you all about it.

All this may sound wonderful. And, in fact, it often is.

But there's a danger that a man (or woman) like this may get carried away with himself, may become involved in a talking marathon, and may tell you a lot of things that are interesting but irrelevant to what you want to write about.

The worst such case I have personally encountered involved a dentist who had invented a successful pain-killing device. I had asked him for an hour and a half of his time. And for a few minutes it seemed as if that would be more than enough. Although it was apparent that he was very busy, he was delighted to see me. I was able to ask only a couple of questions before he plunged into an enthusiastic description of his work.

In fact, he went on at such a rate that, during the next forty minutes, I was able to ask only two or three more of the 40-odd questions I had prepared in advance. Soon I realized that time was running out. So I finally interrupted him and said something like this: "Dr. Jones (a pseudonym), everything you've told me is very interesting. But you've answered only five of the forty-two questions I came in with. I must get answers to the others if I'm to write a story. If you will just answer the questions I ask, I think we can wind up this interview fairly quickly."

It was, of course, a slap in the face. He flushed. But I had made the statement as pleasantly as I could, and it worked. The rest of the interview went off smoothly, and he was pleased with the story.

It's not often that an interviewer has to be this blunt. If an interviewee gets off the track, it is usually sufficient to repeat the original question or to go on to another one. But one way or another the interviewer must maintain control of the interview. In so doing he must walk a fine line between letting the interviewee have his head and following his own prepared list of questions too rigidly. If he goes too far in the first direction, the interview may never end. If he goes too far in the other, he may irritate his man and end up with an article that is lifeless and dry.

There is yet one other way in which an interview can become, if not precisely uncontrolled, at least unproductive. That is if the interviewee has a tendency to make broad, general statements without offering support for these statements. Unless the interviewee can speak with the authority of the Delphic oracle, such a tendency can be very damaging to the interview indeed. For it is anecdotes, examples, facts, and illustrations that bring most written material to life and that render any general observations an interviewee may make interesting and believable.

If the interviewee does not offer these in support of his observations, it is the duty of the interviewer to ask for, even to press, for them. It is not necessary, of course, that every statement an interviewee makes be supported by an example, but enough should be to make the result seem meaningful.

There is another possible problem in connection with conducting an interview. That involves knowing what to do if the interviewee lies. Actually, in my experience, lying is not a common problem. The interviewer may sometimes run across shadings of the truth or self-serving statements, but the outright lie is not frequent.

This, of course, is not to say that it does not occur at all. Some years ago, for example, I had occasion to interview a surgeon about a subject I have now forgotten. The magazine I was working for was also interested in the increasing number of malpractice suits to which doctors were then becoming subject. So I decided to question the surgeon about this and began by asking him if he himself had ever been involved in such a suit, knowing full well that a patient had filed one against him only a few weeks previously. His prompt answer to my question was: No.

It was one of those moments no one likes. I knew he had lied. And he knew that I knew.

Yet I did nothing. After a moment's hesitation, I passed on to another matter.

There can be no easy rule of thumb about what to do when a man lies. But if there were to be one, I would say that, in most cases, disregarding the lie is probably the wisest course. The reason is that, if you call the man's bluff, you will immediately put him on the defensive. And if, to use an old-fashioned term, he fancies himself a gentleman, he may be very embarrassed indeed. The rest of the interview is likely to be tense, awkward, and unproductive. Certainly the man who lies—and is caught at it—will not want to be interviewed by the same person again.

The determining factor as to whether to disregard a lie, however, must be the importance of the question and the answer to the story you plan to write. If they are central to it—or very nearly so—you may well want to make an issue of the lie, especially if you are sure of your facts. Whether you take issue adroitly or bluntly will have to depend on you, the interviewee, and the circumstances in which you are involved.

Even though lying may be infrequent, the experienced journalist soon develops a sixth sense about it. The sixth sense may not operate perfectly, but it operates well enough. The journalist usually recognizes when he is being lied to, even though he may not know what the truth of the matter is.

And if he does not know the truth, he can, of course, do nothing at the moment. In other words, to indicate or even to hint that a man has told a lie, when one does not know the truth, is the height of rashness. If you fall into this self-made trap, you may find yourself in the wrong, in which case you will be the one to suffer embarrassment. The better way is to probe into the suspected lie as deeply and as delicately as possible, then to check the matter later with one or more outside sources.

All the while that you are interviewing someone you are forming some impression of him. Whatever the particulars of your impression may be, you are making an over-all estimate of him as a person—favorable or unfavorable.

If you are a wise interviewer, you will go into any interview with the secret assumption that you will like the person you are to interview. If you are even wiser, you will realize that it does not matter whether you like him or not. You are there to obtain a story, not to strike up a friendship.

Once in a while, however, you will run across someone whom you really feel inclined to dislike. In these cases it is important that you not show your true feelings. This can be easier said than done, of course, for most of us show our feelings more often than we realize. But showing them can set off a subtle reaction in the interviewee, who may secretly withdraw into himself or otherwise fail to provide you with all the material you would otherwise obtain.

There is a way around this problem, however. And that is to concentrate intensely on the subject at hand—or on the article that you plan to write. Stop thinking of the interviewee as a person and regard him as what, in many ways, he primarily is—a provider of information or of opinions. Usually this will do the trick.

Few subjects have been written about less often than closing an interview. Yet closing an interview properly can be even more important than opening it properly. And for several reasons.

For one thing, you may someday want to interview the

same person again, whether you realize that at the moment or not. Leaving him with a good impression of you is the best way to assure that he will be willing to see you again.

How can you do this? Don't allow the interview to run more than five or ten minutes beyond the time you asked for. Of course, if you still have questions you'd like to ask and if the interviewee indicates, tacitly or overtly, that he'll be glad to continue the interview, that's fine.

But if he indicates he has other appointments, don't overstay your welcome. Try to arrange to return another day. Or ask if it will be all right if you call him up and complete the interview on the telephone.

Ordinarily, of course, this problem shouldn't arise. You should have foreseen your needs well enough to know, quite closely, how much time you will need. Whatever the situation, however, it is up to you to bring the interview to a close, barring any attempt by the interviewee to continue it.

Be sure to thank the person you've interviewed for his time and help. And unless he's really let you down, tell him the interview was good. Most people appreciate a brief word of praise about the interviews they give. I've even known presidents of well-known corporations to smile with appreciation when told that they had given an excellent interview.

The reason is simple. Most people have had very little experience with journalists. And at the end of an interview they like to think that they have done well, just as you would if you had undertaken a job with which you had had little experience.

If you know when the results of the interview will be published or otherwise used, say so. If not, tell the interviewee that you will let him know as soon as you can when they will appear.

Also assure him that you'll see to it that he receives a copy or copies. Making sure that he receives the finished product will do more to cement a relationship than any word of thanks or praise you may give.

By the time you have brought the interview to a close, thanked your man, praised him, and promised to let him see the final result, you may be getting up out of your chair or even going through the door. Your notebook will be closed or your tape recorder will be shut off.

Will the interview be over? Usually, yes, but sometimes, no. And the wise interviewer will be very alert to the possibility that it isn't over.

Why might it not be over? When an interview seems to have ended, any tension the interviewee may have felt may disappear. Or he may suddenly remember something he ought to have told you. Or he may let slip some revealing remark that throws the whole matter you have talked about into new perspective.

This kind of thing may not occur often, but when it does you may learn something of great value. It won't be necessary to whip out your notebook and take further notes. Just listen intently and remember what is said. Then write it down as soon as you can.

Whenever this kind of thing does happen, you can be sure of one thing: In the interviewee's eyes you have conducted a successful interview. For people do not pour out information after an interview is over unless they have decided that you deserve their help. And when they have decided that, you have indeed done well.

7. Three Special Problems

Not all interviews take place face to face. Not all involve only one person. Not all are published in a newspaper or magazine or reported through some other medium. For this reason I want to discuss three special kinds of interviews, all of which involve problems that do not usually occur in the course of the standard interview.

One of these special kinds of interviews is the telephone interview. The second is the group interview. The third is the off-the-record interview.

If a general rule were to be established about using the telephone to interview other people, the best rule would probably be: All other things being equal, don't do it. In most cases the telephone interview is simply less productive than the face-to-face interview.

It is no accident that almost all of the top public opinion pollsters in this country prefer to conduct interviews in people's homes—or at least on their doorsteps—rather than by telephone. The pollsters believe that their interviewers can establish more effective rapport with people when talking to them in person rather than over the telephone. And they are right.

In a face-to-face interview the interviewer can be friendlier than on the telephone. He can more readily ascertain how the interviewee is reacting to his questioning. And he can more easily determine the interviewee's meaning by observing his facial expressions and his gestures.

If it is better from the interviewer's standpoint to conduct an interview in person, so is it better from the interviewee's standpoint. If you interview a man by telephone, he isn't able to see you any more than you can see him. In fact, he may not know either you or the organization you represent. For these reasons he may be more reserved in his remarks than would otherwise be the case. And he may be more inclined to terminate the conversation at the earliest opportunity.

It is important to bear in mind that the telephone is an intruder. Your call will come at a time when the interviewee does not expect it. He may be in the middle of an unusually busy day. He may not want to talk with you at all. It will not be as if he had set aside a special time and a special day to hold the interview.

There are still other drawbacks to the telephone interview.

There is a much greater danger that the interview will be superficial and touch only on the highlights of the matter under discussion. This is primarily because the telephone interview tends to be much shorter than the face-to-face interview.

It is also much more difficult to take notes during a telephone interview. You must hold the telephone in one hand and scribble with the other. Usually it is necessary to scribble as fast as you can. The interviewee can't see you doing this, of course, and any pauses in your conversation may seem awkward and strange to him.

Finally, if you want pictures to accompany the story you are planning to write, you will be at the interviewee's mercy, and that is the mercy of an amateur. If he must have pictures taken, you will have to trust his judgment as to what should be photographed and what should not. If he already has pictures on hand, you can only hope that they are what you are looking for.

All of which brings us back to the general rule: All other things being equal, don't use the telephone to interview people. And it doesn't take any reflection at all, of course, to realize that all other things are rarely equal.

So it's no surprise that editors, writers, and reporters constantly use the telephone to conduct interviews. They do so for all kinds of reasons. They may not have the time to give to or to set up a face-to-face interview; they may need information almost immediately. The organizations they work for may not have the money to send them 500 or 1,500 miles for an interview. They may just not want to make the effort. Or they may have only a relatively few questions to ask and may think—rightly or wrongly—that they can adequately cover these questions by telephone.

In short, the telephone is a very important and useful tool in modern journalism. So here are some suggestions on how to decide whether you should resort to it rather than to the face-to-face interview. The suggestions presume, of course, that you have a choice—that neither the pressure of deadlines nor the expense of travel effectively prevents you from even considering a face-to-face interview.

1. How many questions do you need to ask? If you plan to ask more than about eight or ten, in most cases it will be wise to see the party in person. The nature of interviewing itself suggests that a few additional questions may crop up during the course of the conversation. And more than is the case in face-to-face interviewing, people get tired during extended telephone conversations. As a general rule, the

longer the conversations go on the less productive they are likely to be.

To look at the whole matter another way, if you think your conversation will last more than fifteen minutes, give serious consideration to seeing the interviewee in person. In point of fact, the conversation will probably last twenty-five or thirty minutes. And that's long enough for any telephone interview to last—not only from the interviewee's standpoint but also from your own. Telephone interviewing is tiring for the interviewer, too.

2. How long and how important is the article you plan to write? The shorter the article the more likely it is to lend itself to telephone interviewing. If it will run to only two or three typewritten pages, you may easily be able to find out all you need to know by telephone. If it will run to ten or twelve pages, however, it is very doubtful that you can find out all you need to know without seeing your party in person—unless, of course, you plan to use him just to fill in some gaps in your information.

3. How many other people do you plan to interview? If you plan to interview just one man about a subject to which you plan to devote a half dozen or more typewritten pages, be wary of interviewing him over the telephone—unless you are already in possession of considerable background information. You, he, or both of you may overlook matters of vital concern.

If you plan to conduct brief interviews with several men, you are on safer ground in using the telephone. You are less apt to fall on your face if one interview doesn't work out. You are more apt to learn all the important things you should learn. And you are more likely to produce a well-rounded article. In fact, it is safe to say that the telephone is often most useful to journalists when they need to produce a relatively short roundup article that includes information from several organizations or several people.

4. Finally, how complex is the information you wish to obtain? If you will be talking about highly technical matters of which you have little or no understanding, be hesitant to resort to the telephone. A telephone conversation is rarely the place to ask basic, orientation-type questions. If you do ask such questions and if you don't quickly grasp what you are told, you run the risk that both you and the organization you represent will look poorly in the interviewee's eyes. You also increase your chances of making an error.

So, before turning to the telephone, always be sure that you know the fundamental concepts and terminology in use in the field you are inquiring about. If you are talking with a man in person, the situation will be different. It may be possible for him to refer to pictures, charts, and other visual aids to make his explanation clearer.

To sum up what's been said so far: The telephone is a highly useful journalistic tool. But it involves a higher degree of risk than face-to-face interviewing. So it's best used for relatively short interviews on subjects in which the interviewer already has considerable grounding.

When you do use the telephone, here are a few tips designed to help you get the most out of it:

Get to the point right away. In a telephone interview it is best to avoid opening pleasantries altogether, unless you're a personal friend of the person you're calling. State who you are, what you're connected with, and why you're calling. Then ask if the interviewee has a few minutes to answer your questions. If you have no more than four or five questions to ask, make that plain. It will tend to reassure the interviewee that he won't be on the telephone for the rest of the afternoon.

Be flexible. If the man indicates that he's tied up and would like you to call back at a later hour or day, go along with him if at all possible. There's absolutely no advantage to trying to force a person to talk with you at a time that is inconvenient to him. He may decide that he doesn't want to talk at all.

Plot your questions in advance and make them as specific as possible. In an earlier chapter I indicated that I always do this in advance of all kinds of interviews but that many other journalists go into interviews with only a few key questions in mind and still produce successful results. In a telephone interview, however, I don't think there's much room for argument. You must know precisely what you want to find out.

Consider tape recording the interview. Although I'm no advocate of tape recorders in interviewing, I think a much stronger case can be made for using them in extended telephone interviews than in face-to-face interviews. The conversation seems to go much faster in the one than the other. And scribbling, which is often very close to real scribbling, is much more difficult.

A tape recorder can ease both these problems. And if the interview is not too long, having the tape transcribed should not be a problem.

Earlier it was indicated that it is usually wise to ask a man if you can tape-record a face-to-face interview. Whether this is also the wise thing to do in the case of a telephone interview is questionable. If you do tell the interviewee and if he does not know you, the knowledge that you are taping the interview may make him more cautious than ever. Also, he may insist on seeing the results of the interview prior to publication, even though you may be rushing to get it into print.

On the other hand, if you don't tell him, there is a question of whether you are being fair. Some people would consider the taping an invasion of privacy.

The way to resolve the problem is to consider in advance whether you are likely to be talking about embarrassing or potentially embarrassing subjects. If not, then you may do well to err on the side of caution and *not* tell him you are recording the interview. This is especially acceptable, I think, if the interviewee will have a chance to see how you plan to use the material he gives you before you publish it. If you will be talking about subjects on which most men would employ more than normal discretion, however, it is a different matter. Then you will have to consider the circumstances and weigh whether you would be unfair in not disclosing that the interview is being recorded.

Finally, if you take notes instead of using a tape recorder, go over them immediately after the interview. When I conduct a face-to-face interview I sometimes go over my notes right away, sometimes a few hours later, sometimes the next day. After a telephone interview, however, I flesh them out at once, without exception. That is largely because the notes are likely to be sketchier than those I take in a standard interview.

Other journalists of my acquaintance seem to find the same thing. Also, the details of the conversation seem to fade more quickly from one's mind. It is important to combat these drawbacks to the telephone interview at once.

When I refer to a group interview I mean the kind of interview in which one or two journalists interview a number of men or women at the same time. I do not refer to that rare, occasional aberration in journalism in which a number of representatives of the same publication interview just one man at the same time. The latter kind of interview is usually—although not always—a patent waste of time and manpower.

One of the worst examples I have heard of took place within very recent years at the offices of one of the nation's major newsweekly magazines. No fewer than twelve editors sat down with a man who was an expert in a certain area of finance. Each editor was allowed—and expected—to ask just one question. The result was a relatively brief and successful question-and-answer story that could easily have been handled by just one or two editors.

As this anecdote suggests, the results of a group interview that is held by a magazine or newspaper are often presented in question-and-answer form. When well done, this kind of interview can be highly successful because it is apt to be highly readable. If it is handled poorly, however, the resulting story can be very confusing. I have even known instances in which no story resulted at all.

An occasional proponent of the group interview is *Playboy*. Perhaps once or twice a year it assembles a number of experts on some such topic as religion or criminality and asks them to expound their views. The result is presented in question-and-answer form, with, of course, *Playboy* doing the questioning.

And, very frankly, I think the result is often unsuccessful—in sharp contrast, incidentally, to the magazine's one-man interviews. I believe the group interviews are often unsuccessful for a very simple reason. The magazine includes too many interviewees—sometimes as many as eight or nine.

This makes it hard for the reader to keep them all straight. If he is interested in what a given man says, he must often look back to the introduction to remind himself who the man is and what his credentials are. To make a reader keep checking back so as to know what is going on is simply not good journalism.

This and other experiences with the group interview suggest one simple rule for conducting it, presuming you are planning to publish the results in question-and-answer form. Never include more than six men in the group. Five, in fact, are a perfectly acceptable number, and so are four. Three, of course, would seem to be the minimum number to include if it's a group that you are thinking of.

Radio and television, you may have noticed, rarely violate this precept. Almost always they interview no more than three or four men at a time. And yet television at least benefits from the fact that its audience can see the interviewees and more easily remember who is who than it is possible to do when an interview is reported in printed matter.

The problems connected with interviewing several men at once are severe enough so that I would like to suggest an alternative that I have occasionally found quite successful. It is sometimes possible to interview a group of men separately, ask them all the same questions, yet still report their answers in question-and-answer form or something very similar. This approach may work especially well if the interviewer has a chance to check the result with the various interviewees prior to publication.

Nonetheless, this approach can usually work only when your primary goal is to seek information and advice that can be passed along to your readers. If you wish to present a discussion-type interview, in which there may be subtle conflicts of opinion and in which no definite conclusions may be reached, it is almost imperative that you bring the interviewees together. They must be given a chance to thrash out their differences face to face if the interview is to be really successful.

The other rules for conducting a group interview are not really much different from those for conducting a one-man interview. But a few points do deserve special emphasis.

It is probably better to enter such an interview with many fewer questions than you might bring to a one-man interview. A group interview has a tendency to create its own momentum and to get into conversational facets that you may never have thought of. Thus, if you have too many predetermined questions, you may never get to them all.

It is doubly important that the journalist in charge of the interview maintain strict control of it. This is much harder to do than is the case in one-man interviews. The journalist must not only make sure that the discussion never gets too far off track, but, even more important, he must make sure that all the participants have a chance to speak their piece. It is easy enough for one or two eloquent—or voluble— men to dominate an interview if the interviewer does not take care. This can cause hurt feelings and also result in loss of valuable commentary.

Finally, unless the group interview is a brainstorming session whose results will be used primarily as background information by the journalists present, it will probably be most unwise to try to cover it with paper and pencil. It may, of course, be possible to have a stenographer present whose sole duty will be to take down what is said rather than to ask questions or otherwise participate in the discussion. If you can't or don't want to use a stenographer, then you will almost certainly be wise to employ a tape recorder, although the problem of transcribing the results—and of knowing who said what—will be a big one for the typist involved.

The group interview is not common in written journalism. Perhaps that is because of the inherent problems it creates. Nonetheless, when well handled it can be very successful indeed. Certainly, the television networks have proved this time and again, although it is obvious that they operate under much easier conditions in conducting this type of interview than any magazine or newspaper does.

A few years ago a reporter for the *New York Times* appeared in the office of an upper-middle-echelon official of the U.S. State Department and asked to interview him about a certain diplomatic problem of the day. The State Department official said he'd be glad to answer any questions the reporter might pose, provided it was clearly understood that the entire interview would be off the record.

Whereupon the reporter stood up, closed his notebook, and said he could obtain the information he needed elsewhere—and obtain it on the record. And he did. As a matter of fact, he obtained it from a State Department official of higher status.

This incident is not unique. Plenty of reporters refuse to hold off-the-record interviews. And there is a great deal of logic in their refusal. After all, it is a journalist's chief function to produce intelligent, interesting copy. But if he can't report what he has been told, why listen to the telling in the first place—especially if he believes he can obtain the same story from another source?

But before dismissing the off-the-record interview as a waste of time—which it, nonetheless, often is—a couple of comments are in order.

First, if you are ever faced with the seeming necessity of conducting an off-the-record interview, be sure that you and the man you are interviewing understand what the term really means. To most journalists the term means just what it seems to mean: None of the material obtained in the interview may be reported in any fashion whatsoever. The typical layman, however, is not apt to be versed in the ins and outs of journalism. In insisting that an interview be off the record, he may only be saying: "Use the material I am giving you if you wish, but make sure that nobody knows it came from me." In other words, he may be doing no more than trying to hold a background interview, the results of which can be reported without attribution to the source. It is also possible that, although he may seem to want to put the entire interview off the record, he may really be seeking to protect only a few individual statements.

The fact is that even experienced, sophisticated laymen aren't always knowledgeable about the niceties of journalism. Thus, shortly after the Eisenhower Administration first came to power, Secretary of the Treasury George Humphrey held a luncheon for some of Washington's financial reporters. The new Secretary talked rather freely about some of the trouble he was having in persuading the Pentagon to hold down its requests for more money.

Without having so specified, he assumed that the entire luncheon was off the record. But the reporters assumed no such thing. They believed that it was a "background lunch" and that they could report what they learned, provided they did not attribute it to Humphrey.

And in fact a number of them did report it. One of them was a personal friend of mine. Humphrey just happened to see his story in print first, called him in and gave him a strong tongue-lashing. It was not the first time that a man new to the power corridors of Washington had not understood the ground rules of journalism.

Second, before rejecting or condemning off-the-record interviews out of hand, remember that different journalists work in different environments. Some operate in situations in which off-the-record interviews are held much more often than elsewhere.

This is certainly the case with the Washington press corps. Its members sometimes hold such interviews—occasionally unexpectedly—at lunches, dinner parties, and in other less social circumstances. Why do they agree to this?

One answer is that they sometimes have to. The officials with whom they talk may function at such a high level of government that they can dictate their own terms. And in some instances these officials may prefer the off-the-record interview to a background interview.

Another answer is that they may not wish to alienate a useful source of information. The official who insists on talking off the record today may be quite willing to talk on the record a month or two hence. But if he has been rebuffed in the first instance he may turn to another journalist than the one who turned him down.

Finally, nothing precludes a reporter from following up on an off-the-record interview. In other words, even though he hasn't obtained a useful story from such an interview, he may have obtained a useful lead. He may be able to go to other sources, verify what he has learned in the off-the-record interview, and write a story that in no way involves the man with whom he first talked.

The off-the-record interview is not confined to Washington. Crime reporters, for example, sometimes hold off-the-record interviews with police officers. In some such cases the information the reporters obtain is off the record only temporarily.

Thus the police may know certain facts about a murder or some other crime that they have not yet solved. For one reason or another they may not want these facts revealed to the public before the crime is solved. But they may tell trusted reporters what they know—with the clear-cut understanding that the information cannot be reported until a later date.

This brings up the one rule that can be flatly and unequivocally stated in regard to off-the-record interviews. Once you have agreed to interview someone on this basis, keep your word. You will probably never get another interview from the person if you don't.

Otherwise, no rules can be given for this kind of interview—only questions that must be asked. The individual journalist will have to answer them in light of the circumstances in which he finds himself.

Does off the record really mean off the record?

Could you obtain the information you seek from somebody else?

Is the person you are interviewing someone with whom you are likely to have a continuing relationship and from whom you might obtain on-the-record stories in the future?

Does the interviewee have seemingly valid reasons for wanting to talk off the record?

Finally, do you operate in an environment in which the off-the-record interview is, if not commonplace, more frequent than in other areas of journalism?

You will have to be fair and discreet in answering these questions, but there's no need to be ridiculous. Some men have tried to put entire press conferences off the record, even though as many as 250 people have been present. The experienced journalist scoffs at such naïveté. And well he should. What is off the record when only one or two men hear it is hardly off the record when 250 people do so.

8. The Right of Review

Late in 1966 Jacqueline Onassis—then Jacqueline Kennedy, widow of President John F. Kennedy—brought suit against Harper & Row, the book publishers, and *Look*, the biweekly magazine. The suit was designed to prevent the publishers from bringing out a book about the assassination of her husband and the magazine from printing a serialization of the same. The book was entitled *The Death of a President*.

The suit, and all the events surrounding it, produced front-page newspaper headlines and a spate of magazine cover stories all over the world. One famous American magazine said it involved "the book of the decade" and "the crime of the century."

Whatever the merits of the suit, the facts are fairly plain. The Kennedy family, and Jacqueline Kennedy in particular, had agreed to help William Manchester, a onetime reporter for the Baltimore *Sun* who had already authored one book about President Kennedy, to write another, dealing with his assassination in Dallas, Texas, on November 22, 1963. If Manchester was not what is known as an official biographer, he came about as close to it as it is possible to come. Among other things, the Kennedys agreed to grant him interviews and access to written materials that they denied to other authors, some of whom had equal or bigger reputations. Mrs. Kennedy, in fact, told another would-be chronicler that she had "hired" Manchester to write the book in order "to protect President Kennedy and the truth."

For his part, Manchester agreed to let the Kennedys review his book prior to publication. This permission to review, in fact, was included in an 11-point contract that he and the Kennedys both signed.

Although the precise meaning of this right of review was not spelled out in most of the magazine and newspaper stories about the suit, the implication was clear. In the Kennedys' opinion, and apparently in the opinion of many other people who were also involved, it meant that the late President's family had the right to change or to delete any passages that they wished to. And exercise that right, if that's what it was, they definitely decided to do.

Several old friends of the family, including some who had been politically close to the President, first read the book and suggested some changes. Apparently these changes were primarily designed to rid the book of certain seeming prejudices against President Lyndon B. Johnson, Kennedy's successor. And apparently Manchester agreed to make most of the changes.

Then the book's magazine serial rights were sold to *Look* and complications began to develop. The Kennedy family was concerned that the serialization might distort certain passages in the book. Yet in selling the right to serialize the book Manchester had granted *Look* editorial control of his material.

In the meantime Mrs. Kennedy herself had read at least certain portions of the book. Four months after the late President's assassination, she had let Manchester interview her for periods totaling ten hours. The interviews had been tape-recorded. And now, upon reading the book, she felt that he had reported her emotions and inward feelings too faithfully, and she became determined to blue pencil certain passages she did not like. Naturally she ran into some resistance from Manchester, Harper & Row, and *Look*.

Whereupon she obtained a temporary court injunction blocking publication of both the book and the serialization. Her basic charge was that Manchester had broken their contract.

Ultimately the case was settled out of court. Both book and magazine serialization reached print—but only after certain other changes and deletions had been made. Thus it was reported that *Look* had agreed to delete some 1,600 words of its 60,000-word serialization and to soften or otherwise change certain other passages to which Mrs. Kennedy objected.

Judging from all the reports of the case, many misunderstandings developed on all sides. But whatever else may be true, this much seems sure: William Manchester made a mistake in the very beginning by agreeing to let the Kennedys review his book, especially since that permission apparently carried with it the right to command changes and deletions. As Theodore H. White, author of *The Making of the President,* an even more famous book about President Kennedy, put it, "A man who writes on public affairs should refuse to commit to anybody the right to review his copy."

This whole story brings up a problem that often confronts magazines and, to a lesser extent, other journalistic media in more subtle and ambiguous form. The problem is simply this: Should journalists voluntarily check their stories with the sources from whom they obtained their information, in order to assure the stories' factual and, possibly, interpretive accuracy? In thus stating the question I am assuming that when they do thus check their stories journalistic media do not grant, and do not intend to grant, any contractual right of review such as was enjoyed by the Kennedys. Rather, they are merely seeking factual corrections and any other suggestions the sources may want to make. They are not relinquishing their right to reject the suggestions and possibly even the factual corrections if they so wish.

This is an important point. It is important partly because it is the way in which all or nearly all magazines that presently follow this policy do operate and partly because it is the only sensible way in which to operate.

Newspapermen rarely have to face this issue. They almost never submit copy to the sources of their stories prior to publication. A major reason is that, unless they are writing the kind of feature story that can be held up for a few days, they don't have time. Today's news must be printed tomorrow.

To be sure, newspapermen will sometimes telephone the source of an article to double-check the accuracy of certain facts and figures that they have been given. But this is a far cry from checking out a whole story.

In many ways it is well that newspapers do not often face this problem. More than magazines, more than radio and television, they are the chief defenders of this country's freedom of the press and of the public's right to know. Even when a contract granting the right to review does not exist, submitting copy to the source of a story runs the inherent risk that the source may attempt to censor the copy. And no believer in freedom of the press wants that. It is better that misstatements of fact sometimes creep into newspaper pages—and many more do than are ever acknowledged—than that the newspapers submit to outside checking.

Why, then, do many magazines follow the policy of checking out their stories before going into print? The magazines would reply that they seek total factual accuracy. And, ironically, many old-line newspapermen would scoff at them. They would argue that any editor or writer who can't get the facts straight in the first place doesn't belong in the field of journalism.

Like many other arguments based on pride or contempt, this one is only partially true. Although it may be more than half true, it is surely not the whole truth.

Obviously, it is incumbent upon any journalist worthy of the name to get his facts straight. And most of them do, most of the time—probably almost all of the time. They wouldn't last long in their profession if they didn't.

But it is hard to imagine that there is any journalist alive who has not made some misstatement of fact in some story, somewhere, sometime. Whether the misstatement was trivial does not matter. It has been there.

Sometimes the fault for errors of fact rests with the journalist himself. He may have misread or misheard. Or he may have failed to check information that he should have checked.

But to say that the fault may sometimes be the journalist's is not to say that this is always the case. A source the journalist relied on and had good reason to rely on may have given him erroneous information. Not deliberately, but through a failure of his memory. Dates, figures, and other kinds of precise data often fade from people's memories or are remembered erroneously.

Speaking in a somewhat different context, Sir Winston Churchill once put the problem very neatly by saying, "During my life, I have often had to eat my own words, and on the whole I have found them a wholesome diet." Although journalists do not have to eat their own words very often, just about all of them have had to munch on one or two.

So there is solid reason for checking out copy with its sources prior to publication if you are in a position to do so. Factual and other kinds of errors do creep in. Anyone who has ever edited other men's articles or sent them out for checking can attest to this.

In fact, many leading magazines insist on this policy. *Reader's Digest* is a notable case in point.

Many well-known individual authors do the same thing. Stewart Alsop, the onetime newspaper columnist who subsequently wrote for the *Saturday Evening Post* and who now writes for *Newsweek*, is certainly one of the most distinguished, respected journalists in the country. Yet in his book *The Center: People and Power in Political Washington*, he unabashedly concedes in two different instances that he has submitted whole articles to outside sources for factual checking.

Thus, in 1962, he collaborated with another journalist to write an article for the *Saturday Evening Post* about the Cuban missile crisis. The article dealt in particular with all the debates that went on within the Kennedy Administration on how to handle the crisis and with the final decision on how to prevent the Soviet Union from planting further missiles in Cuba.

To write the article Alsop and his coauthor had to draw on many sources, some secret or semisecret. To make sure that they had reported the whole story correctly, they submitted it to President Kennedy himself. Thus, Alsop writes, "Kennedy read the piece for accuracy and proposed a couple of minor changes."

The other instance involved a chapter in *The Center* itself. The chapter dealt with the nature and state of the Defense Department. To write it, Alsop interviewed the then Secretary of Defense, Robert S. McNamara. Among other things, Alsop and McNamara discussed nuclear war, and Alsop wrote that McNamara had said, "It's extremely important to realize that a full nuclear exchange could destroy both sides."

Subsequently Alsop asked McNamara to check the chapter for accuracy. In *The Center* Alsop writes, "The paragraph above came back unchanged, except that the 'c' in the word 'could' in the last sentence was crossed out and a 'w' neatly substituted."

A small change, a tiny change, but an all-important change. Important not only to the accuracy of Alsop's book but also because of the indication it provides to the whole thinking of Robert McNamara, widely regarded as the most influential member of the Cabinets of both President Kennedy and President Johnson.

Ensuring factual accuracy is the overriding reason for submitting articles to sources. But sometimes there are additional benefits to be derived from this process. For example, upon seeing an article a source may suggest the inclusion of additional information that did not come up during the course of the interview on which the article is based. Occasionally such additions may add real value to the story in question. Or a source may suggest a minor deletion or change in wording that will save some person unnecessary embarrassment, yet not cause any damage to the story.

Personally, I believe that the case for checking out articles is much stronger than the case against it—all other things, including the nature of the publication one works for, being equal. But plenty of publications do not check out their articles, often as a matter of principle. And there's no question that there are risks involved in doing so.

The chief risk has always been indicated. Pressure, occasionally amounting to something akin to attempted censorship, can and sometimes is brought to bear to change wordings, delete passages, or even kill articles outright. I don't believe that such extreme pressure is common, but it does occur.

I know of one instance in which a company president decided that he did not wish to release the contents of an interview he had given. The issue in which the interview was to appear was already on the presses, however, and the editor told him nothing could be done. Happily, the editor was the kind of man who would have told him nothing could be done anyway.

Pressure—and I mean pressure, as opposed to politely worded requests—can also take the form of threats to withdraw or withhold advertising. Again, this kind of pressure is not common. But it does occur. And it can be tougher to withstand, because the threat may be transmitted to a publication's sales (advertising) department rather than to its editors. By and large, sales managers are not well known for standing up for editorial integrity when advertising is threatened. It is no accident that Harold Ross, *The New Yorker*'s most famous editor, strictly forbade any advertising space salesmen to even set foot on the floor where the magazine's editors were located. He enforced the ban, too.

There are no easy rules for resisting this kind of pressure. Much depends on the particular circumstances, on the attitude of the sales manager involved, and more importantly, on that of the publisher. Some publishers have strong scruples about not interfering with the work of editors they trust. Other publishers have even stronger scruples about not interfering with advertising revenue.

The most common kind of pressure to force changes in editorial copy comes through force of personality. Instead

of returning an article by mail with whatever factual corrections and suggestions he may have, a story source calls an
editor up and, in effect, tries to browbeat him into making
certain changes that are neither necessary nor called for.

Some editors and reporters can stand up very well under
this kind of pressure. Others tend to buckle. Two or three of
the latter kind have asked me on occasion how to handle
veritable demands for changes in their copy. And I have
always recommended the same course: Tell your source
that you will jot down his requests, then pass them on to the
editor in chief. After all, one of the top editor's jobs is to
handle the hot ones.

A good editor or reporter does not pass on many things
like this, however. Normally he should be able to handle
requests for changes himself. It's his job, too, to protect the
independence and integrity of his own publication.

I still vividly remember what I hope is the only instance
in which I submitted to pressure for unnecessary changes in
editorial copy. The article discussed so-called venture capital firms. In essence, these firms provide start-up or additional capital to new, little businesses that seem to have
good ideas and good executives but not enough capital with
which to get going. Often the little businesses are operating
on the technological frontiers of American industry.

Partly for this reason, venture capital firms constitute an
important factor in the American economy. But they are
not well known because they guard their operations with a
great deal of secrecy. There are only about ten or a dozen
of real consequence, and I had been fortunate to get in to
see three of them.

Upon seeing the article I had written, the president of
one firm called up and said it looked fine. Five minutes later
the vice-president of one of the other firms called to request
four or five minor changes involving perhaps a total of a

dozen words. The changes seemed justified, and I agreed to make them.

Although I thought the conversation was over, it wasn't. For the next forty minutes the vice-president talked on, indicating a vague, general dissatisfaction with the article. I was puzzled. I tried several times to find out what was bothering him but couldn't seem to pin him down. He didn't seem to have any other specific changes to request.

Finally, however, the nature of his anxiety became somewhat clearer. He told me that the article would have to be cleared by his firm's tax lawyers before he could agree to the release of the information pertaining to his firm. (To the best of my knowledge, his firm was doing nothing wrong, but I later learned from another person that the vice-president feared that the article would somehow lead to an investigation by the Internal Revenue Service.)

It was late on a very hot Friday afternoon in late May. By the time the vice-president finally came to the point I was tired and out of sorts. Reluctantly I agreed to his request. And no sooner had I left the office than I knew I had done the wrong thing.

On Monday morning I returned to the office. I didn't bother to take the matter up with the editor. Instead, I immediately wrote a letter to the vice-president. I made it as courteous as I could and told him that we would stand by the few minor changes I had agreed to make. In fact, I added, we would be glad to consider any others he might want to suggest provided there were sound editorial reasons for considering them. But under no circumstances, I emphasized, could we let his tax lawyers review the article, especially if that was to mean that they had veto power over it or any of its parts. To do so, I pointed out, would be to surrender the editorial independence of our own magazine.

I never heard from the vice-president again. And I do not imagine that he heard from the Internal Revenue Service either. In any case, the article was published, and his firm is still in business.

Although actual pressure to change articles is not common, requests for changes are. Sometimes the requests are fully justified. Sometimes they are not justified at all.

Some people make their requests deferentially. Some make them matter-of-factly. Some make them abruptly. Some request the change or deletion of only one or two words in a 25-page article. Others request sweeping changes in whole paragraphs or even in whole pages.

The worst offenders are those rare people who make only a few changes in a long article, yet insist on retyping the whole article before returning it. It is then necessary for the editor to compare the retyped article with the original one, line for line, in order to determine what the requests are.

How can an editor determine whether it is right to make requested changes or not? There can be no easy, quick answer to this question. So much depends on the nature of an individual article. But asking yourself these few questions may help you come to a decision:

How many requests are there? It is safe to say, as a rough rule of thumb, that the more requests for changes a person makes the more cause you have to suspect that he has engaged in what some editors call doodling. That is, he has sought change for the sake of change. This presumes, of course, that the changes do not involve corrections of factual errors.

Of course, there are always exceptions to this general rule. I know of one case in which a corporate official requested twenty changes in a 20-page article. Although all the changes were minor, only three or four of them involved factual matters. The magazine in question made all of them, however, because all of them seemed justified.

This brings up a second key question: How valid are the reasons for the requests?

Some years ago I had occasion to interview Charles Brower, chairman of Batten, Barton, Durstine & Osborn, the advertising agency, and several other company chairmen on how they had gone about picking their successors as presidents. Brower is a very droll man, and the interview he gave me was frequently punctuated by my own laughter and that of his public relations director.

Among other things I asked him was how important a man's wife was if he was under consideration for a company presidency. His quick retort was that a wife should be given no consideration at all, so long as she was "white and presentable."

If anyone else had been in the room, he would have known without any question that there was not the slightest trace of racial prejudice in Brower's remark. As a matter of fact, I included it in the article I wrote without even thinking about that possibility.

Back came the article, however, with the request that this statement be deleted. Upon seeing it in typewritten form, Brower believed that it could be interpreted as evidence of racial prejudice. And what would have made it all the worse from his standpoint, his public relations director told me, is that he had been active in the civil rights movement and had gone out of his way to recruit Negro employees for his own firm.

I didn't like making the deletion because businessmen don't often make colorful or even semicolorful remarks. But I made it. There is no point in embarrassing a man unnecessarily. Besides, the remark was not necessary to an understanding of the point Brower had been trying to make.

Many requests for changes, other than changes in fact, involve matters like this. That's why it is often wise to find out the reason for the request.

Do the suggested changes improve the article? There is little point in acceding to them unless they do, presuming, of course, that they are not made with the thought of saving someone from unnecessary embarrassment.

How is the request made? The occasional person who abruptly demands changes as though this were his God-given right is given short shrift by most editors I have known, other things being equal. And well he should be. The chance to see an article before it goes into print is not a right, but a privilege.

Finally, what is the background of the person making the request? The more experience a man has had with the press the less consideration he should be given. For example, men who enter politics have sometimes made statements to journalists that have had unfortunate national repercussions and that, in retrospect, they probably wished they had never made. In short, they have committed bloopers.

In most such cases I doubt that they had a chance to review what they said before it went into print because they were dealing with newspapermen. It may seem unfair that a man who goes into politics does not usually have a chance to change or retract unfortunate remarks before publication. But that is one of the prices one pays for going into politics.

And, considering the nature of our political process, it is probably just as well. Surely one criterion by which to judge a political candidate—although not necessarily the most important one—is how well he handles questions from the press. The man who frequently blows his cool, as the saying goes, or doesn't think before he speaks may commit serious indiscretions in dealing with foreign nations. In this connection I have heard it said that one reason President John F. Kennedy was so successful with journalists was that he rarely answered a question without first thinking how his answer would look in a headline.

But most people don't go into politics. And most don't deal frequently with journalists. And if a man has in good faith given a good interview—in which he has made one blooper that he would like to change—I believe that he deserves consideration.

That does not mean that his request should be automatically granted. Much depends on what he said, why he said it—and in connection with what article. But it does mean that his request should be looked upon with more sympathy than that of someone who often deals with the press and who knows, or should know, the risk he takes in making rash, ill-considered remarks.

These are the questions one can quickly ask himself before acceding to any requests for changes other than changes in fact. Yet the best way to deal with the problem of requested changes is through preventive action. The reporter or editor who sends out an article for checking should make plain that in so doing he is not giving the source of his story editorial control over it. One way to do this is to ask for "corrections of any factual errors there may be and other *suggestions* you may have." Some people won't take the hint. They'll still act as if they had a right to change the article as they see fit. But most people will take it.

Early in this chapter it was indicated that newspapers do not often let outside sources review their articles prior to publication. Yet they sometimes do submit to a more general kind of censorship, under which they agree not to print any news at all about certain matters for indefinite periods of time. Sometimes this semicensorship is more or less imposed from without. Sometimes the newspapers and other journalistic media impose it on themselves.

During wartime, for example, newspapers, radio, and television sometimes withhold news for days, weeks, or even months through fear of jeopardizing military operations. And during recent race riots the news media have sometimes delayed or limited their reports through fear of inflaming the passions of both blacks and whites.

This kind of review is beyond the purview of this book. But it does re-emphasize the importance of all of journalism in our society and the heavy responsibility resting on each of its members. And that is really the subject of the next chapter.

9. The Job Is Yours

Some years ago two friends of mine were employed by the same magazine. Although it had a sizable staff of editors and writers, it often assigned my friends to the same story. This surprised me because, like other magazines, it usually expected one man to handle any given story by himself.

One day I asked one of my friends the reasons behind the special arrangement. "It's really quite simple," he said. "I ask more and better questions than Pete does. He doesn't have quite enough brass. But he's a better writer. So, when we handle a story together, I ask most of the questions, and he does most of the writing."

It might be nice if more journalistic chores could be handled in this two-platoon fashion, but usually they can't. It might also be nice if journalism required less interviewing, but it doesn't.

To be sure, there are jobs in journalism and allied fields that require little or no interviewing. But these jobs are in the minority, and they are rarely at or near the top of the editorial totem pole. The man who would climb upward on this pole must learn to interview people successfully, if for no other reason than that interviewing is at the very heart of all journalism.

The ability to interview can be cultivated and mastered. No doubt, some men and women are, through inheritance or instinct, better interviewers than others. But whatever gifts they have must be developed. And those who have lesser or seemingly lesser talents can certainly develop those that they have to the fullest. In short, two old clichés do apply: To a considerable degree, interviewers are made, not born. And practice does make perfect.

This book has tried to emphasize a number of qualities and steps essential to good interviewing. Thus it has stressed the importance of being a friendly human being, of showing enterprise in seeking interviews, of preparing in advance of an interview whenever possible, of knowing how to record an interview both by tape and by paper and pencil, of maintaining control of an interview, of listening to the interviewee with uncommon care, and so on. But there are two other qualities that a good journalist often needs if he is to be successful as an interviewer.

One is persistence. Occasionally an interview can be obtained through tactful persistence when all else fails. This is most likely to be the case when a journalist is trying to interview someone of considerable stature.

For example, in 1968 the Columbia Broadcasting System featured what was unquestionably one of the most successful and interesting interviews ever held on television. The interviewers were Martin Agronsky and Eric Sevareid. The interviewee was Hugo L. Black, the aging senior Associate Justice of the U.S. Supreme Court.

Any journalist who had managed to interview Black about anything would have achieved a considerable feat, if only because Supreme Court Justices are notoriously reticent with the press. But to persuade him to appear on an hour-long television show and to discuss some of the Court's most famous and controversial decisions was a real coup. Later Agronsky confessed that it had taken him four years to persuade Black to appear. In short, persistence did pay off.

Another quality the good interviewer often needs is imagination. As was suggested in an earlier chapter, it has only been through an imaginative approach to some of today's hippier actors and actresses that some journalists have been able to get them to start talking.

Take another example of imaginative interviewing—one from a newspaper's sports pages. In 1967 and 1968 Yale University boasted one of the Ivy League's all-time great quarterbacks—a young man named Brian Dowling. In 1968 he led his team to a one-sided triumph over Dartmouth in a game that was watched by 50,000 people in person and by many more on television.

Figuring perhaps that many of the people who were interested in the game were already familiar with its highlights, William N. Wallace, a sportswriter for the *New York Times*, devoted only a few sentences to detailing the scoring and the statistics in Sunday's newspaper. Instead, he devoted most of his 25-paragraph story to an interview with Dowling. In the interview the quarterback explained the thinking and action that went into seven of the most important offensive plays Yale made during the game. It was an imaginative kind of story to do under any circumstances and especially so as a replacement for a routine account of how the two teams had trudged up and down the playing field.

Surely it would seem unnecessary to mention that a journalist also has a responsibility to be honest, whether he is interviewing someone or performing some other professional task. But apparently this assumption is not necessarily correct.

Not so long ago *Newsweek* reported that the Radio Corporation of America had provided some 1,400 radio stations across the country with taped mock interviews with several prominent entertainers, such as Carol Channing, Duke Ellington, and Henry Fonda. These stars had recorded answers to certain questions. And disk jockeys at the 1,400 radio stations were able to ask and record the questions suggested by these answers. To help the jockeys to do the job right, RCA had provided them with scripts that suggested how to word the questions. In short, the announcers were able to create the illusion that they had actually interviewed the entertainers. Of course, they had really done no such thing.

Disk jockeys are not journalists. They are not even on the fringes of journalism. But the stations that employ them are in the field of journalism if only because they carry news reports. And *Newsweek* reported that an executive with one New England station had openly bragged that many listeners had "swallowed the interview ruse hook, line, and sinker."

Incidents like this should serve as sufficient reminder to any journalist or any person allied to journalism that he has a personal responsibility to maintain the highest standards of integrity in all that he does. Fortunately, there are signs that many journalists take this responsibility seriously.

For a number of years the Columbia University School of Journalism has published the *Columbia Journalism Review*, a quarterly devoted to reporting and commenting upon the best and worst examples of current journalism. And not long after the close of the 1968 Democratic National Convention several dozen Chicago journalists banded together and, among other things, began publishing the *Chicago Journalism Review*. Angered by what they considered pressure from their own publications to suppress unfavorable convention news about Mayor Richard Daley and Chicago policemen, the journalists determined to improve professional standards and publicly condemn obvious breaches of journalistic ethics.

If morality doesn't urge such concern on all journalists, practicality should. Journalism has its enemies. It always will have.

Lately, however, this enmity has sometimes seemed to know no bounds. During the convention cited above, some two score journalists required medical attention. Most of them had been attacked by the police, who seemed particularly interested in preventing photographers and television cameramen from recording both the riots and the action the police took against the rioters. A few of these journalists were severely beaten. Although this is the worst incident that comes to mind, it is not the only time in recent years that journalists have been physically attacked while trying to do their jobs.

Usually, of course, enmity against journalists takes a subtler form. Courts, corporations, and government agencies on the federal, state, and local levels deliberately withhold information that would be of benefit to the general public or to certain individual publics to know. Whenever a journalist is barred from seeing official records or from interviewing certain people there is a question as to whether the American people are not the losers, assuming, of course, that national security or some similar good is not involved.

Certainly journalism in general, and newspapers in particular, are in the very front rank of those who can, do, and must protect many of our fundamental freedoms and the nation itself from tyranny, corruption, and dereliction of duty. And certainly the chance to report unfavorable news, without fear or favor, is one of journalism's strongest weapons.

But if journalists are to open all the doors that they should open and receive all the cooperation that they would like, they must do even more than they have done to keep their own house in order. The greatest accomplishments in this area will not come through committees, new and improved codes of ethics, or the commentary of critical journals. The greatest accomplishments will come through the day-in and day-out actions of individual journalists who believe that their calling is high and their responsibility great—to themselves, to their employers, and to their publics. The journalist who is as honest, as fair, and as responsible as he knows how to be will accomplish more than any group within or without the profession.

As this book has suggested again and again, interviewing is the bedrock of journalism. If editors, writers, and reporters had to rely solely on written records and on what they saw with their own eyes—if they could not seek the face-to-face opinions of people, great and small—journalism would not be half so interesting, important, or influential as it is today.

Yet it is well to keep matters in perspective. Interviewing can be overdone. Interviews can be held too often. And they can be conducted with the wrong people.

Jack Gould, the highly respected television and radio critic of the *New York Times,* brought home this point very vividly in a column he wrote following the 1968 political conventions. Chiding the three major television networks for their coverage of the Democratic convention in particular, he wrote:

"Both the Columbia Broadcasting .System . . . and the

National Broadcasting Company were so bent on staging their own show that the viewer was deprived of hearing the full range of disagreement over the Vietnamese war plank, to cite only one example. . . . The two chains providing gavel-to-gavel coverage became rattled and relied excessively on their floor reporters, who interviewed and reinterviewed delegates to the exclusion of the business of the convention. . . .

"The networks themselves need to be more careful and restrained. For too many hours at a time the viewer might easily [have decided] that the anchormen and floor reporters [were] the substance of a convention, rather than the delegates and candidates. There is a bolt loose somewhere when the familiar faces of [Walter] Cronkite, [Chet] Huntley and [David] Brinkley, and Howard K. Smith are on camera more than the people ostensibly making the news.

"The whole concept of omnipotent anchormen has had the effect of coming between the viewer and the event in which he is interested. TV's conceit that it is invariably more interesting than what is being said on the podium is simply not true. The viewer has some rights in arriving at these judgments for himself, and the function of TV is then to provide unobtrusive background material."

Thus the wheel comes full circle. Early in this book I indicated that it was important that you impress the people you interview as a decent human being. I also stressed that it was important that you not overemphasize your own role in your interviews and that you put the person you interview and his opinions ahead of your own feelings. If you will do these two things—and if you will master the relatively simple techniques that I have mentioned elsewhere—then, presuming that you have any talent for journalism at all, I do not see how you can fail as an interviewer.

Index